Splendor of Sorrow

*Through a life of spectacular adventure and searing tragedy,
Eddie Doherty came to see in the Seven Sorrows
of the Mother of God how God's light shines
even in the sufferings of this world.
In these pages, he takes you into those Sorrows,
showing you how to find the mystery
of divine joy within them.*

Eddie Doherty

Splendor of Sorrow

What a Hard-Boiled Crime Reporter
Discovered about the Love of Jesus and Mary

SOPHIA INSTITUTE PRESS®
Manchester, New Hampshire

Sophia Institute Press®
Box 5284, Manchester, NH 03108
1-800-888-9344
www.sophiainstitute.com

02 03 04 05 06 07 08 10 9 8 7 6 5 4 3 2 1

Contents

⁀

Splendor of Sorrow

Christ asks you to share His sorrows

Blessed be God, who has sealed my eyes with blindness. May His name be honey in mouths and hearts forever. Through His mercy, I see clearly. Darkness does not dim or blur my vision. Sight does not distract me. Tears do not disturb me. And, because my horizons have been narrowed, such things as time and space no longer hamper or confine me.

What is space to me? A snare and a delusion, a hindrance, a multiplicity of lies, a labyrinth I am unable and unwilling to traverse fully, a myth because it is invisible and incomprehensible, a reality because it impedes my steps, a blackness filled with an infinity of sounds and smells and objects partly shaped through which, at times, I grope. I shut it out of my consciousness at will. It does not concern me. It does not exist.

And what is time? When the loud noises of men cease, and the slight noises of God are heard — the sighing of the wind that is His breath, the rustle of leaves, and the murmur of waters beneath His feet — then I know that it is night, that the stars and the moon are shining, and the mercy of sleep has come to heal the world. Yet the night is the same to me as the day, and as full of the wonders of God as is the dawn.

I sleep, and I wake, and another yesterday is gone, gone farther from me than the yesterdays of my youth. In a few moments of the present I may live ages of the past, or of the future.

In the hushed hour Christ spent in the Garden of Olives, He lived and suffered all the years of man. Time passed that night as it does now, scattering its mysteries of birth and pain and joy and death throughout the world; yet time lay still, and tamed, and quivering at His knees, that night, to be sheared of its black sins.

It was the hour for the Son of God, the Son of Man, to take upon Himself our sins, that He might expiate them.

A leaf twisted against the silver of the moon and fluttered from its branch. Christ piled a thousand years of horror on His shoulders ere that leaf found rest upon the ground — all the idolatries, the lies and lusts and greeds and hates, the prides, the persecutions, the murders, the bestialities of man.

A dog barked, and before the sound had ceased re-echoing in the night, all our sins until that hour had been combed out and added to the shameful load that He must carry to the Cross.

He blushed, seeing Himself, covered with the rags of our degradation, as His Father must see Him. He blushed until the blood forced its way through His burning cheeks like sweat. And He cried out that the chalice was too bitter. He could not drink it. He cried, "Your will be done";[1] and heard the whisper of a loved one plotting to betray Him with a kiss!

His shame and His horror are more awful than all the stripes awaiting Him, than the ugly thorns, than the nails that will fasten His hands and His feet, than the spittle and the jibes and the blasphemies that will assail Him — than even the tears of His mother.

My dull eyes see this clearly each time I visit the garden. I kneel, out of the moonlight, close to His sleeping apostles. I look at Him. And He looks at me and at my time — this little period of eternity men call *now*. And there is no barrier of years between us, between my now and His then. They are the same moment.

[1] Cf. Matt. 26:39.

Splendor of Sorrow

My skin crawls with fright for the things I have done to cause that bloody sweat. My arms tremble. Words crowd into my mouth in such haste and confusion they are meaningless. My tongue tastes evil. And I blush, even as He does, seeing myself as I must look to Him.

He rises and walks to His apostles.

Once He showed Himself to them transfigured so that His face shone like the sun and His garments were white as snow. Once He shared with them the ecstasy of His Father's voice, and the rapture and the glory and the fire and the love of the Holy Spirit.

Now, in His desolation, He would share with them the love and the pity and the sorrow He feels for men — and seek the comfort of their human sympathy. But they are asleep. And Jesus goes from them and kneels to pray once more, alone.

I would crawl forward, to pour what little sweetness I might into His appalling draft, to wipe His face, to speak of my contrition, to tell Him of my love. But I dare not. I would wake His apostles that they might minister to Him. But I cannot. And I would weep — but the salt sweet ease and warmth of tears have been denied me.

Blessed are they who weep with Jesus in His Passion, and with Mary in her sorrows. Theirs is the peace of souls washed clean by love and soothed by pity. They are comforted not only on earth but also in heaven; for, when she sees a face bright-wet because of her, or of her Son, does not the Queen of Heaven rush to kiss the tears away?

And blessed are they who grieve but do not cry, who are too strong for tears, or too weak, or too ashamed; for grief enriches all who squander it on others.

Yet blessed too are those, like me, who wish to cry but cannot; for the tears of the saints are ours to beg — and to offer as our own. Saints dead a thousand years or more are glad to give their tears to a blind man born centuries after their advent into Heaven.

St. Francis of Assisi, a little brown man with great rubies glowing in his palms, lends me his tears in Gethsemane. St. Francis, watching and praying a stone's cast from his Love, observes the pitiful confusion of my mind and speaks to me.

"Draw near," he bids me. "Be not afraid. Did you not hear Him calling to His Father as confidently as a little child, though He was covered with the slime of centuries? He waits for you to speak. Say to Him, 'Lord, I am sorry, forgive me, teach me to love You!' Say to Him only, 'Lord Jesus, O my love!'

"What's stopping you? Two thousand years? Time does not exist for Him. He will be here always, until the end of time, waiting for men to come to Him. Must He wait forever, abandoned as you see Him now?"

The apostles turn uneasily in their sleep. But they do not wake. And the bloody sweat breaks once again through the cheeks of the holy face.

"Draw near, my son," St. Francis says once more. "Do you not know He will not be outdone in love or generosity? Do you not know that if you take one step toward Him, He will come a hundred steps toward you?"

Francis is weeping now; and I crawl forward on my hands and knees. And, oh, the riches that are mine!

I do not visit the garden often, nor can I stay there long. These eyes that pierce the fogs of time and space cannot endure His agony. Nor can my soul endure its weight of guilt nor bear the joy that floods me when He lifts me from the earth.

But I walk frequently near our Lady. Saints pilot me. Saints talk to me of her. Saints show me a thousand splendors. And sometimes they work miracles of grace for me; and soften her sorrows, or turn them into joy.

St. Martin de Porres, a Dominican lay brother beloved of Jesus, Mary, and Joseph, a humble black man and the most marvelous of all the saints I know, leads me each night into the Temple of Jerusalem that I may witness the drama of the Presentation, a play so beautiful I never tire of it.

We watch it, kneeling side by side, sometimes near the great bronze altar with the smoke of sacrifices rising from it, sometimes by the golden table with its twelve loaves of bread, sometimes by the seven-branched candelabra carved out of a single piece of gold, etched with almond branches in full blossom, and topped with little oil lamps. Sometimes there is no scenery at all; and only the glow of Martin's beautiful black face lights up the scene.

The First Sorrow:
The prophecy of Simeon

Mary helps you rejoice
in all aspects of God's will

Outside the Temple gates there is the haggling of many tongues, the smell of animals and fowls, the traffic in turtledoves and heifers and goats and lambs, the changing of money, the business of the world.

Inside the courtyard hundreds of Levites, massed on the marble steps, cry *Hosanna* to God with voice and psalter and cymbal and lute and harp; priests make their ablutions in the water of the great laver that rests on the backs of twelve gold oxen; guards pace the flags with heavy steps; and pilgrims pray audibly as they bare their feet.

Within the Temple there is peace, the fragrance of incense and of prayer, the hushed footsteps of the priests, the coo of a pigeon, the bleat of a snow-white lamb beneath the sacrificial knife.

St. Joseph and our Lady enter quietly, humble people, poorly dressed, with the dust of a long hot road upon their garments. Joseph has an offering of doves in his right hand; and Mary, in a fold of her blue robe, carries the Hope of the world.

They are lowly people, yet exalted above all humankind. They have talked with angels and heard their voices singing. Mary, a virgin, has borne the Son of God, and they have held Him in their arms and kissed Him. There is in their eyes the look of seraphim forever chanting, "Holy, Holy, Holy"; and in the bearing of our Lady there is the surge and the thunder and the exultation of the *Magnificat*.

"My soul magnifies the Lord, and my spirit has rejoiced in God my Savior. Because He has regarded the humility of His handmaid; for, behold, henceforth all generations shall call me blessed!"[2]

The glory of the Annunciation is still in her; and the overshadowing of the Holy Spirit — how could she have endured such divine rapture, this sixteen-year-old girl? — and the wonder of Elizabeth's greeting; and the feel of the Child in her womb, growing with her blood and stirring in His sweet retreat; and the miraculous birth of the Baby in the stable at Bethlehem; and the

---

[2] Luke 1:46-48.

first deep look into His eyes; and His first smile; and the first tugging of His tiny mouth upon her breast.

How lovely her little feet — reverent and slow as befits the holiness of the Temple, yet with a wild dance in them, a dance of purest joy such as her ancestor David danced before the ark.[3] How soft her shining eyes that have never mirrored sin. How beautiful her mouth that prays when it says, "My Son!"

Joy sings in all her veins, untarnished, undimmed, undiluted by any thought of fear or sorrow. And the greatest of joys awaits her, for she has come to present her Child to His Father!

"Like any mother taking her first-born home, she comes," says St. Martin. "To show Him off with pride, in her old home. This was her home, this Temple. Here her mother and her father gave her up to God. Here she learned of God, and of the Scriptures. Here bright angels came to gossip with her of the Lord. Here she met and married Joseph.

"This is the house of her Father, the great Lord God Almighty. This is the home of her Spouse, the Holy Spirit.

---

[3] 2 Sam. 6:14.

"In a moment her Father and her Spouse will look upon her Son. And He on them! A family gathering unparalleled in Heaven or on earth; a situation created by divine omnipotence before the morning star; a moment scarcely bearable even to the Dominations and the Thrones. They are holding their breaths in fear and awe."

Mary and Joseph are standing before the altar, and the priest has come in his immaculate white robes; but there is neither awe nor fear in Mary or in Joseph. There is only sublime happiness, intolerable joy.

"She is a lamb," says Martin, "a spotless white ewe lamb."

And I am chilled, remembering the knife of the priest. And I call to her, "O Mother, don't be so happy. It breaks my heart to see you so. Prepare yourself for your first sorrow. A knife is reaching for your heart!"

She does not hear.

The ritual has been finished. The birds have been offered up, and their blood spilled toward the Holy of Holies. The priest is walking fast away, unaware of the miracle he has helped to bring about.

And Simeon is coming, little gold bells tinkling on the hem of his robe.

Mary helps you rejoice in God's will

Simeon is seamed and slow and bent with the weight of the onyx stones on his shoulders and the breastplate of jewels hanging on its golden chains. Little gusts of air, stirred by the feeble motions of his head and the shaking of his hands, ripple his white beard.

His eyes are filmed with weariness and age and longing — longing for the serenity of the grave his life has earned, and for the sight of Israel's Salvation. His lips are thin and bloodless, and ever in motion, shaping little prayers. Yet there is beauty in him, and majesty, and a great benevolence. The smell of incense and lilies walks with him, and wisdom guides him; for he is filled with the Holy Spirit.

Simeon is coming, groping his way through thoughts of God and the Redeemer He has promised. And Mary goes to him, smiling, and places the Child in his arms.

His dim eyes brighten. His body stands erect. His purple and scarlet garb no longer drags against his shoulders. His voice bursts into exultant song.

"Now do You dismiss Your servant, Lord!"[4]

He has seen the Son of God, and cannot wait to die. His words bring wonder to the two who gaze and listen.

[4] Luke 2:29.

"A light to the revelation of the Gentiles, and the glory of Your people, Israel."[5]

"Joseph does not understand," Martin whispers. "And Mary is rapt in a beatific dream. The favorite daughter of Almighty God, the spouse of the Holy Spirit, and the mother of Christ, has forgotten, in her joy, the reason her Son was born. Because of the fragrant mists of love in which she has lived so long, she has not yet glimpsed the Cross."

Simeon returns the Child into Mary's outstretched arms. He lifts his hands in benediction. And he speaks to the Virgin softly.

"Behold, this Child is set for the fall and for the resurrection of many in Israel, and for a sign that shall be contradicted. And your own soul a sword shall pierce, that out of many hearts thoughts may be revealed."[6]

For a moment Mary wavers. Her hands, her dear white hands, press Jesus quickly and fearfully closer to her. The blood drains from her face. Her mouth is tortured, and a swift breath whistles inward through her lips.

[5] Luke 2:32.
[6] Luke 2:34-35.

But she does not falter. She does not protest. She does not weep.

Joseph, troubled in mind and soul, moves closer to her; knowing by love alone that a blade is quivering in her heart. His eyes are as filled with pain as hers.

"The mists are blown away," says Martin, "the hideous Cross is raised upon the hill, and her Son hangs on it, dying. All the prophecies in Holy Writ are racing through her mind —

" 'He shall be led as a sheep to the slaughter. . . . For the wickedness of my people have I struck Him. . . . He was wounded for our iniquities, He was bruised for our sins. . . . They have pierced my hands and my feet. They have numbered all my bones.'[7]

"All the prophecies since God bade Abraham to sacrifice his Son!

"On this spot, on this Mount Moriah where the Temple now stands, Abraham built an altar, and bound his son, and took the sword to sacrifice him to the Lord.

"Here, perhaps on the very spot where the altar stood, stands our holy Mother, offering the same sacrifice to God. An angel stayed the sword of Abraham,

---

[7] Isa. 53:7, 8, 5; Ps. 22:16-17.

and God provided a ram to be slain and burnt in place of Isaac.

"But no angel shall stay the destiny of Jesus, nor God provide a substitute of any kind for Him.

"She knows this now. She knows now what it means to be the Mother of God. Yet she stands straight and staunch, a valiant queen, accepting the command of God — and willing it with all her heart."

"Willing the crucifixion of her Son? For such as us?"

"For such as us, even for those who will spit on Him and curse Him and butcher Him to death."

Simeon has gone, to spread through all Jerusalem the glad news of the Redeemer. The Levites are singing *Hallelujahs*. And Mary and Joseph are leaving the Temple, as slowly and as reverently as they entered. But their feet stumble. Their shoulders droop. Their heads are lowered.

"It was cruel of Simeon. Why did he do it?"

"Cruel? You called to her to prepare for this sharp knife, and gave her but a moment. Simeon has given her more than thirty years. His words cut deeply — yes. But have not words of yours and mine cut deeper?"

"But to strike her such a blow! In the moment of her intensest bliss! I cannot bear it, Martin. Call her back.

Say something, do something. We cannot let her go like this."

Martin calls to her, and she turns. She comes to us. Her long eyelashes gleam with silver brine, and there is a tear upon her cheek, a tear much lovelier than the loveliest star or any other sight my blinded eyes have seen, or imagined that they saw.

"O Mother," Martin says, "comfort this child who wishes he could comfort you. Let him know the thoughts that sustain you in this fearful hour.

"Tell him it is the will of God your Son must die for us; and therefore, your will. Tell him the will of God is stronger in you even than your love of Jesus. And more holy.

"Tell him that only through pain and anguish, borne willingly for the love of God and His holy will, shall you, and he, and I, and all your children, find any real or lasting joy.

"Tell him that only through the Crucifixion, impossible as it seems, shall any of us, including you, find true bliss.

"Tell him there will be more joy in Heaven and earth, and in your own heart, sweet Mother, through the death of Jesus, than there was in His birth."

Splendor of Sorrow

Mary answers not a word. She gives her Baby into Martin's arms — as reverently as do our priests at the altar when they place Him on the tongues of the faithful.

And there is a smile upon her face.

Ah, who would not be blind, to gaze upon such splendor?

The Second Sorrow:
The flight into Egypt

⌒

Mary gathers your sorrows
and showers you with joy

The ass plods slowly through the sand, breaking the silence only with his tired breath. Joseph coaxes him to a faster pace with friendly words and soft caressings; but the beast does not respond.

"Rest, then, a moment," Joseph bids him. "We must not overtax your strength. We have sore need of it."

Joseph has walked a hundred miles or more through sand and dust and flinty stones and clinging brush and brier. Blistering heat he has endured, and blinding sandstorms, and freezing night winds, but there is no weariness in him, nor thirst, nor hunger, nor the need of sleep. There is in him only fear, and ache of heart, and boundless responsibilities. And love.

He looks at Mary and the Child, and there is comfort for them in his face, and a holy wonder. Mary looks at him with pity, noting the sag of his strong shoulders, the droop of his arms, the heaviness in his head. She watches him chafe his hands. They must be numb with the cold. Even she, forced to wear his heavy mantle above her robes, has felt the lash of the desert night wind.

The Child stirs in her arms, and she bends her head to His. The red-gold moon that has followed them all through the night haloes their two heads. And the stars that wheel above them, so bright they seem covered with frost, swoop low to see their Maker.

His head rests against her breast. Her breath stirs the fine silk of His hair, making it glitter. His breath blows on her neck. His sweet, warm, thrilling breath.

O infinite wonder of God! His breath blows on me, too, each morning and mingles with my own — the breath of Christ that quickens all my life.

But there is no Holy Communion now. He has not yet willed us His body and His blood. He is a Child flying into Egypt, stealing at night through a desert empty and lonely as a church. There is no church, except the shaggy beast that carries Him, no tabernacle save His mother's arms, no sanctuary lamp except the moon, no congregation except the Archangel Michael and the poor blind man whose cane He guides.

A night bird calls, and Joseph tenses. A hare is tangled in a distant bush, and dust rises up like smoke.

Fright catches in Mary's throat, and she hugs the Baby fiercely. Every shape has menace in the night. Every rock may be a soldier. Every tree may shelter Herod. Every bush may harbor robber or wild beast. Every hill of sand may cover sacrilege in ambush. And every sound bears terror.

"It is nothing, " Joseph says, "We must go on. But the beast is overladen."

The load is not too heavy. A loaf of bread. Two skins of water. A little skin of wine. A few handfuls of dates wrapped in papyrus. A strip of cloth that serves as shelter against the blast of the wind and the fury of the sun. Those who travel with Jesus travel lightly.

I look for the gifts of the Magi, the gold, the frankincense and myrrh. But they are missing. Perhaps the gold has been given to the poor. What need of gold have they who hold the Treasure of the world? The myrrh has been rubbed into His little body, and the incense burned to Him in prayer.

Joseph unties the skimpy tent, shakes the dust from it, and rolls it into a bundle for his back. The water skins he ties about his neck and shoulders. The dates go into a pocket. There is only Mary and the Child to carry now. And the bread and wine. Joseph adjusts the water skins, and whispers to the beast.

And as we follow, the angel and I, we hear our Lady singing a lullaby. Her voice is soft and sweet, softer and sweeter than St. Michael's. Soft and low and infinitely sad.

> "Sleep little Lamb without stain;
> Dream of green pastures in May.
> Herod shall seek You in vain:
> Angels are guarding Your way."

"He is filling Himself with the Virgin's milk," the angel says, "and soon will fall asleep."

I do not see the angel. I see only the gleam of the sword he carries, perhaps the same sword Adam saw in Eden. An arc of fire in the dark; a burning symbol, flaring bright, or dimmed and faintly smoking.

Adam and Eve, driven out of Paradise, could never have felt the anguish of Mary and Joseph driven from their home. Even as she sings to soothe the Infant Jesus, there must be boundless sorrow in Mary's heart.

The words of Simeon must be stabbing her afresh: "A light to the revelation of the Gentiles — for the fall, and for the resurrection of many in Israel — a sign that shall be contradicted, and your own soul a sword shall pierce." And the words that Joseph heard from Heaven:

"Arise and take the Child and His mother and fly into Egypt — for Herod will seek the Child to destroy Him."[8]

To destroy Him! To destroy Jesus!

Only a day or so ago the Magi came, wise kings following a star, kings of the Gentiles traveling from far off to adore Him. Only a day or so ago friends and neighbors came also to adore and give Him little tokens of their love.

"And all through the centuries," says the angel, interpreting my thoughts, "those who love Him will give Him little things, prayer, renunciation, sacrifice, thoughts — gifts finer than any the Magi carried."

Only a day or so ago there was peace, and holiness, and the dearness of familiar things and customs, the soil of the prophets, the Temple wherein Father, Son, and Holy Spirit rejoiced in One Another — and in Mary and Joseph. And there was safety for the Child as well as love and adoration.

Now they must go furtively through the night, the first refugees of His Kingdom, into a nation of men who worship gods of wood and stone, a land made fertile by the tears of Israel.

[8] Matt. 2:13.

Splendor of Sorrow

Mary has read of Egypt in the Scriptures. She has read of Pharaoh, and how he would not let her people go. And she has read — how often? — of the first Passover. And of the blood of the lamb that was sprinkled on Israel's doors.

O Mary, the blood of a Lamb!

> "Dream of green pastures in May.
> Angels are guarding their God.
> Dream not of Pilate, I pray.
> Dream not of nail, thorn, or rod."

Men would destroy Him — men whom He loves so much. Even now they would wrest Him from her breast, drive spikes through His baby hands and feet, and fasten a crown of thorns upon His dreaming head. But His hour has not yet come.

He will go back to Israel sometime — to men as cruel as Herod. His own people. His mother's people. They will spill His blood. And He will shed it willingly. For Israel? Ah, Israel will reject Him. Israel will cry, "Crucify Him; crucify Him." Israel will shout, "His blood be on our heads."[9] He will die; and He will leave Israel. And Israel will harden its heart and let Him go.

[9] Cf. Matt. 27:23, 25.

And what of Israel without Him? His mother's people; His own people?

Desolation of desolations. A wound too wide and deep for tears. An ache beyond all thought of aching.

"Where are the other angels?" I ask.

"All about us!" says St. Michael. "And Joseph leads the way, more blessed, more trusted, more burdened, more privileged than any of us. My task is easy. I guard the rear. But Joseph — Joseph will labor till he dies, spending his whole life for Jesus!"

His sword is raised and lowered at the name. Silver trumpets sound among the stars, and music quivers on the black-grey desert floor.

"To work for Him, to feed Him, to clothe and shelter Him, to hold and kiss Him, to guard Him constantly, to teach Him all the things a man should know — what angel is worthy of such honor?"

"And to die in His arms, and Mary's," I add. "What man could ask for more?"

"Or wish for less? If I could envy, I would envy men. How much more important to God you are than we — even the worst of you! The angels who sinned were cast forthwith into Hell. Men who sin — why, the Almighty woos them!

Splendor of Sorrow

"It was not for us the Son of God was made flesh, to be tortured and defiled and slain. It is not to us the full infinity of His love is offered. Be glad you are a man."

As he speaks, another sound drifts down from the cold and blazing stars, a sound that sets my knees to quaking, that freezes my spine, that roots my feet in the sand and jerks at all my muscles.

Faint and far away a woman screams in anguish.

"What is it?"

"A woman wailing over the corpse of a baby. A mother crooning to a murdered child. A woman tearing her hair and rending her clothes. A woman cursing God for the sins of men.

"It is Herod writing his name in the blood of babies. It is Rachel weeping for her children . . . because they are no more. It is the woe of Mary's children, thrusting new keen daggers into her heart.

"One of the Magi told her — the Ethiop king. Tarrying a day behind the others, he saw the massacre, and hurried, frightened, toward his home. He passed but yesterday.

"He rides a proud swift camel covered with gold and silver trappings. The King of Kings is carried on an ass!"

"You sent him to her?"

"Would you have women wailing anywhere on earth, and she not know? Would you have children martyred for her Son and keep it from her? Of course I led the king to her feet that he might tell his news. Is she not the mother of those women, and of their slaughtered babies? Is she not the mother of all men — to whom they go, poor banished children of Eve, to whom they send up their sighs, mourning, and weeping in this valley of tears!

"She was born to hold your sorrows, Blindman.

"Sorrow is gold in the kingdom of Heaven. Mary takes all that is offered, treasures it in the vaults of her heart, and issues against it coins a thousand times its value — coins of solace, love, and joy. Pity is golden too, and love beyond all price.

"If Rachel could know that every waking hour of every day our Lady sees the Cross, watches her Love die in agony and shame — and wills Him so to die — would she not think her own woe slight? Would she not drop, on the crossed swords of Simeon and Herod, a stream of golden pity? And for that pity, would not the Mother of Mercy give her serenity and joy?

"Our Lady of Sorrows, Blindman, is a treasure house of joy."

Splendor of Sorrow

"I ask no joy," I answer, "save that of weeping for her. And for the Child, because of all that lies before Him. And for St. Joseph, who is so brave and strong and fine and uncomplaining nobody ever sheds a tear for him. But I cannot weep. I must seek holy eyes to cry my grief for me."

"The tears of saints are far more precious than an angel's paean of joy, and you offer them as your own?"

"Since they are of my contriving, they are mine. Therefore, I offer them. And I offer now to our sorrowing Mother, the tears of Sister Thérèse of the Infant Jesus, the Carmelite nun we know as 'the Little Flower.' "

"Offer them, Blindman," a woman whispers, "for they fall like rain on flowers."

She is kneeling at my side, a woman with a God-hungry mouth, with blue eyes wet — yet parched for the sight of Jesus — and eager fingers holding a crucifix to her bosom.

A nun whose beauty shakes the earth!

"You see my Lord," she says, "and Mary and Joseph. How blessed of God you are!"

Her voice rises to a chant. "O God, my God, for You do I watch at break of day. For You my soul has thirsted, and in how many ways, my flesh. In a desert land where there is no way and no water; so in the sanctuary have I come before You, to see Your power and Your glory. For Your mercy is better than life; my lips shall praise You."

Michael blesses her with his sword, and she turns again to me.

"I cannot see Them, Blindman. Tell me how sweet my Jesus is, how fair my Lady Mother, how dauntless my St. Joseph. Is she looking at Him, adoring Him, taking Communion from His mouth of honey? Is He sleeping in her arms, all warm and rumple-haired and safe? Or does He stir and see us in the dark?"

"See for yourself, dear Flower." St. Michael lifts his flaming sword on high. The whole East catches fire. The red moon pales. The stars take fright and vanish. And the blazing sun leaps up from the horizon.

The ass has halted on a little hill of sand, head hanging as limply as his tail. Joseph is putting up the tent in the shadow of a rock. And Mary is making a bed for the Child, arranging white cloths beneath Him on the ground.

The brown nun rushes toward them, chanting a litany of love words and dropping flowers that root in the barren sand. Trees rise about the Holy Family, trees rioting with red and white and purple blossoms, trees full of winged flowers singing. Lilies scamper over the burning landscape, and tiny white flowers with petals and patterns more wondrous than the filigree of snowflakes. And white and red and yellow roses. Cool flowers dripping silver dew.

St. Joseph, hammering a tent stake into the earth, leaves off his work and goes to meet her. But Mary stands aloof, staring at the crucifix in the nun's right hand.

"O Mother of my Love, my Spouse, my God," the Carmelite cries, throwing herself at the Virgin's feet, "look not so fearfully on this cross. Lady of Sorrows, Morning Star, Refuge of Sinners, Cause of Our Joy, this is the scepter of the King of Kings, the symbol of His power, the memorial of His Love."

She holds it so that the sun chips from it sparks of gold and crimson; so that it flashes more brightly in the glare of day than Michael's sword at midnight.

"This is the hope and the love and the pride and the safety of all your children. This is the sign in which your Son shall conquer. O Rose of Sharon, Gate of Heaven, Queen of all Saints, look tenderly on this cross."

There is dust on Mary's robe, dust on her hands and her face. It is powdered gold in the sunlight. Unshed tears on her long lashes shine like sea-foam shot with sun.

There are tears in the eyes of the Little Flower —
tears that mother glad blue flames.

"It is the symbol of His death, and your unutterable
pain, O Mary, Mother of Martyrs. But it is also the symbol of His victory, and your unutterable joy — for He
will come back to you. Out of the tomb He will come.
Alive. In His own body. Never to leave you again.

"And because of His death, the Holy Spirit shall
come to you once more in love and fire.

"Twice blessed are you, Mary full of grace. Twice
shall you be the Mother of Jesus. Twice shall you be vis-
ited by the Holy Spirit. O Mother of my Heart, look joyously upon this cross."

The tears are gone from Our Lady's eyes. And there
is a smile upon her face — such a smile that my heart
swells and no breath stirs within me.

How pale the beauty of the nun becomes against
that smile! The pallor of a distant star against the rising
moon!

"O Mother of God," my stilled heart cries. "O Mary,
Mother of men! Why am I here, alone of all your living
children? Why is not this desert filled with those who
love you, so that I might share this ecstasy and pain, this
taste of Heaven? Why must I bear it all?"

Splendor of Sorrow

St. Thérèse, more affected than I by our Lady's beauty, snatches words haphazard from the Song of Songs:

"O most beautiful of women! My love, my dove, my perfect one. Your neck is as a tower of ivory, your eyes like pools in Hesebon. Your head is like Carmel. How beautiful you are! How comely! You are all fair, my love. There is no stain in you."[10]

Our Lady takes the cross, as I go toward her like a hungry child. She holds it for a moment against her breast. Rose petals fall from it like drops of blood upon the kneeling nun. Winds blow them from her. Across the arid desert. Across the whole wide world.

Our Lady returns the cross and stoops to wrap her Baby in a linen sheet. And now she stands erect, and turns. And the Child is in her arms, awake, and smiling at Thérèse.

I see Him for the first time clearly. I see Him. I see Jesus!

The supernal beauty of Our Lady dims, as the moon dims in the presence of the sun. And Joseph and Thérèse fade into shadows; while I am transfixed and dying from the shafts His glory hurls.

[10] Song of Sol. 5:9, 2; 7:4, 5, 6; 4:7.

"Oh, let me hold Him, Mother," I hear the nun's voice saying. "Let me hold Him in my arms."

The angel whispers, "Ask Mary the same boon. She loves to put the Infant in the arms of those who ask. That is her greatest joy. If you love her, ask her for the Child."

Thérèse is holding Him, holding Him tightly. And she is murmuring His name: "Jesus, Jesus, Jesus." Hers is the voice, now, of a little girl who cannot contain herself, who must cry out, or swoon from too much joy.

"Your breath is sweeter than all the flowers of earth or Heaven. Your flesh is softer than the petal of a rose, more precious than the world and the sun and the moon and all the stars Your Father made. Your eyes — ah, little Jesus, Your eyes looking into mine, and Your sacred heart beating against my heart — how can I say how dear You are to me?"

I watch Him twine His arms about her neck. I watch His head move up against her shoulder. And then I see Him stretching out His arms to me.

Aye, even to me, He stretches out his arms.

The Third Sorrow:
Jesus is lost in the Temple

God favors those He loves
with sorrows that lead to joy

The Holy Family vanishes along the road to Egypt. The light of Michael's sword flicks out. The Little Flower thrusts a long-stemmed rose into my hands, saying, "Thank you, Blindman, for the gift of God," and hastens back to Heaven. The desert dwindles — disappears. And I am kneeling in some silent church — or tapping my slow course through crowded highways — or sitting on a bench near playing children — or lying snug in bed, far, far from Egypt.

Two thousand years have passed like half an hour. Thérèse's rose has shed its petals and become a cross that holds a silver Christ. The thorns I clutched in poignant recollection of a crown, have turned to beads beneath my fingers' pressure. And time and space close in, to taunt me with my loss.

Gone is the wonder of St. Joseph, my Lady's beauty, and the glory of my Lord. Gone on to Egypt.

Splendor of Sorrow

And I am here in exile? No! My Lord abides in me and I in Him. For I am Egypt, holy ground, a land made fruitful with the Nile-floods of His love, the soil on which His feet first toddled, that heard His baby words and saw Him weaned.

I am the temple of the Holy Spirit. I am the tabernacle of my Savior. His blood pumps through me as it once pumped through His mother.

I am a very heaven. God the Son and God the Holy Spirit meet in my flesh with love beyond all telling. Angels and saints attend Them there, and Mary, Queen of Heaven. And where They are, can God the Father be so far away?

My soul has known the intimacies of God. And my poor body. And neither time nor space — nor death itself — may dim the splendors of my darkness.

Yea, I am Egypt, a new Eden. And I am Bethlehem and Nazareth, and all the towns that ever held the Son of Mary.

Yet, as Eden perished at the angry voice of God, so does my Paradise dissolve within me at the voice of St. Martin, an anguished voice that shrieks, "They have lost Jesus!"

He stands before me in his much-patched habit, panting, sobbing, beating his breast, and dripping sweat and tears. His beautiful black face is twisted with his pain. His nostrils labor with the intake of deep breaths. His mouth is tortured to a comic leer; his voice a mimic cry to make one quake with mirth.

How close our laughter is to tears; and tears — how close to laughter!

"Impossible," I try to soothe him. "No man can lose Jesus. Does He not watch the flight of sparrows? No man escapes Him, Martin; none can lose His love and mercy."

I speak thus to him who was so close to Christ and Mary, this worker of a thousand miracles, this humble man who walked the earth in blinding glory! I, a common worm, speak thus to St. Martin! But then I have not seen him weep 'til now, and I must comfort him.

"It is Mary who lost Him," Martin answers. "Mary and St. Joseph. They cannot find Him. He has gone!"

So Eden dies. And there are dust and ashes in my mouth — and the holy name of Jesus. And we are plunging through the dark and narrow aisles of old Jerusalem, and Martin tells his story.

"They had come up from Nazareth with friends and kinfolk for the Passover in the Temple. The feast had ended, and they started home; Mary with the women and Joseph with the men, each thinking Jesus with the other.

"Behold her, Blindman, in her queenly walk — talking of babies and the care of them, talking of births and marriages and deaths in Galilee, talking of husbands and the things they like for dinner, talking a little, listening much and always thinking, 'Jesus.'

"A word of comfort to a widow. A word of wisdom for a bride; and another for a girl engaged to marry. A crooning note to soothe a fretful infant. And every moment thinking, 'Soon I'll see Him!'

"Thinking, 'Now that He is twelve, and by our laws a man, it is fitting that He walk apart from me with Joseph.' Thinking of the love the Boy bears Joseph. Thinking how, unconsciously, He captures every gesture of His father, to reproduce it later as His own. Thinking, 'He will be tired and hungry and all but choked with dust.' Thinking how sweet to wash His face and hands and comb His hair, how wonderful to hear His prayers — and kiss Him while He sleeps. Thinking, with a stab of pain, 'How fast He grows into a man — to leave me!'

"And Joseph listens to talk of politics and war and crops and taxes, offers his opinions slowly, and often stops to shade his eyes, and seek the dust that marks the caravan of women, thinking, 'How dull life is without Him and His mother!' Thinking, 'He will fall asleep at dinner, and I will take Him in my arms and carry Him to bed.' Thinking, 'It is not much farther; I shall see them soon.'

"The caravans of men and women meet at dusk. Joseph and Mary rush to find each other. The dull, aching day is done. Now they can be together with their Jesus. And, oh, the sharp heartbreaking joy of seeing Jesus!

"But He is gone. He is not in the camp. No one has seen Him!

"That was last night. They have not found Him."

Jerusalem is gorged with revelers and pilgrims. Long caravans are streaming through its gates, long lines of noisy moonlit shadows moving homeward. Light seeps — with drunken singing — from the wine shops. The streets are thronged with reeling, laughing people; and here and there a squad of Roman soldiers go their way, light glinting on their short swords and their armor.

"Look," cries Martin. "In the street. That man and woman!"

A frail old man. A slender woman clinging to his arm. I see them walking with unsteady steps, unmindful of a chariot speeding toward them, a splendid gleaming vehicle of war. They neither see nor hear the danger, nor heed our shouts of warning.

The chariot plunges roaring forward, the horses pawing lightnings from the pavement, and someone crying, "Caesar! Make way, make way for Caesar!"

People are scurrying to safety up and down the street, all except the old man and the woman; yet by some miracle of chance they do escape the hoofs and wheels that might have killed them. They do not feel the wind of passing murder, nor smell the acrid dust it raises, nor hear the curses of the Roman driver.

"Are they both blind and deaf?" I wonder.

"Aye," Martin answers, "blind and deaf, and drunk with sorrow. Behold St. Joseph and our Lady!"

These spent and dazed and shaking figures? This red-eyed greybeard, Joseph? This haggard, half-demented woman, Mary?

The old man speaks to me, his voice so hoarse I scarcely make out his words. "Have you seen Jesus? We have lost Him. A Boy of twelve. A Boy so beautiful the birds sing where He passes. And flowers bloom — to wither when He goes. The children swarm about Him. All men stop to look at Him and love Him. Only yesterday we had Him. And now — we cannot find Him.

God favors those He loves

"A Boy who wears a long, white, seamless robe. A Boy with long gold hair. With hair sun-bleached three shades of finest gold. With silken hair that falls in curls to His wide shoulders. A Boy whose eyes look through you to your heart and make it dance with rapture. You must have seen Him!"

"What color are His eyes?" I ask. "Please, what color are they?"

The old man shakes his head. "Why, I don't know. I never noticed. What color is God's glory? That is the color of His eyes."

Yes, this is Joseph, aged in a day beyond all recognition. Shrunken, enfeebled, etched deep with furrows in his face, shaking in a spasm of dry sobs. And this is Mary, the tears so heavy on her lids and lashes that she cannot raise them!

"Jesus!" she calls. The name sounds in her mouth sweet as the ringing of cathedral chimes. But it is mournful music, a passionate lament, an epic dirge.

She listens.

Bawdy music answers from a tavern.

And now she lifts her blind wet face to Heaven.

"My God, my God, why have You forsaken me, Your mother?"

Splendor of Sorrow

The emptiness of heart her cry discloses! The desolation of her soul that prayer reveals!

Fingers of steel clamp tight upon my entrails, opening, shutting, twisting, reaching for my heart. O God, if I could cry!

"Father, remove this chalice from me," Mary whispers. "I cannot drink it. Lord my Father, Father of my Lord, His Father, surely it is not yet His time. He is really not a man. He is only a little boy. I still sing him to sleep at night. I still watch over Him by day. God, give Him back to me, I pray. But be it done to me according to Your will."

And they are gone, two shadows mingling with other shadows in the moon-specked street, elbowed and shouldered by the careless throngs, two shadows crying, "Jesus!"

"Blindman, they cannot stand the toothed edge of this sword," says Martin.

Jerusalem rocks with his pity, the hard, loud sobbing of a simple child.

"It cuts, not cleanly like the swords of Simeon and Herod, but with a cruel and most unnatural motion. It rips and tears while it pierces. It tantalizes as it wounds. It stops its torment for a moment — that shadow may

be Jesus! Then it begins again with fiercer, more excru-
ciating pain — the shadow is not He.

"This is the deadliest of all the swords, for Jesus is not
there to help them bear it. They have lost Him. They
have lost Him, and they think Him dead!"

In my own time and place I know He still is living. I
know He will be found on the third day. But I am in Jerusalem in my Lord's twelfth year. And all I know is —
He is lost, and even Mary cannot find Him.

And I, too, think Him dead. Some beast has killed
and mangled Him. Some man has slain Him, out of
malice. A robber would not kidnap Him for ransom —
who came to ransom us — for He is poor; and all who
love Him most are poor. Some drunken soldier may
have stabbed Him. He may be, at this moment, hanging
spread-eagled on a cross, beset by vultures!

Are these His mother's thoughts as well as mine?
And Joseph's?

"Lost," I cry. "And all the world lost with Him. Lost.
Inevitably damned! It cannot live without Him. His
church will never be. There can be no priests, no sacraments. Learning will die. There will be no monks to
keep it nourished. There will be no hospitals for the
poor, no schools, no free asylums, no Christian charities

of any kind on earth. There will be only wretched serfs and cruel masters; only slavery and war and degradation; only ruthless murder, famine, pestilence, and death. And, worst of all, the holy name of Jesus will never bless the lips of men!"

This thought I cannot bear.

"Not so!" I shout. "If He be dead, then I shall never die. I shall go down the ages with His name upon my lips for all to hear and worship. I shall forever tour the world to say how Jesus loves us."

"Oh, you will die," says Martin. His sobs have ceased. His voice is steady. And something of serenity is looking through his eyes. "He has made death a glorious thing, an open door to Heaven. But look, Blindman, at this cross."

The sharp corners of his crucifix are pressed deep into his palms.

"This is a Man upon the Cross, and not a little Boy.

"Christ could not die this early, leaving the world without the sacraments, the rivers of His grace, the arteries of His saints. Summon the blessed to seek Him."

I call their names as in a litany.

"St. Augustine, find Him. Great St. Albert, find Him. St. John Chrysostom of the golden mouth, St. Jerome, St. Thomas, find Him. Holy doctors, search the

Scriptures. They may tell you where to find Him. For our holy mother, find Him. Come and tell me when you've found Him. St. Anthony, finder of all lost things, find Him."

Down from Heaven they came trooping, light as snow on snowdrifts falling.

"St. Christopher, the friend of travelers, find Him. Damien, hero of the lepers, find Him. Good thief on the cross, St. Dismas, find Him.

"St. Ignatius, black-robe general, search through all Judea for Him. Send your Jesuits out to find Him: Francis Xavier, Aloysius, Francis Borgia, all your legions."

St. Ignatius gives me courage. "Love will find Him. Love has ever, and will ever, find Him."

"If you love our blessed Lady — "

"Every saint in Heaven loves her. Every saint owes Heaven to her. In her name, command all Heaven."

"Then take charge of all the saints, Ignatius. Send them where you will, but find Him. Have compassion on our Lady. All last night she walked this city. All this day and half this night. Without food or sleep or rest or shelter. Please, Ignatius, find Him quickly."

Friars and monks of all the orders; bishops and cardinals and laymen, popes and peasants, kings and beggars hurry out to look for Jesus. Some I know but most are strangers. Francis de Sales and Don John Bosco, the Curé d'Ars, with Philomena, Brother Joachim the Trappist, Brother Van, and Brother André, leading armies of Yankee warriors. There's Ed Mattingly.

There's my father. There are women I loved dearly. There are my three little sisters, bringing the babies and the children.

There are virgins, wives, and mothers; queens and countesses and peasants; girls from factory, shop, and office; actresses and nuns and nurses; all the radiant saints of Heaven crying to me, "We will find Him."

St. Bernard I send to Mary.

"Walk with her," I bid him. "Try to comfort her and Joseph. Say to her your *Memorare:* 'Remember, O most gracious Virgin!' Call her 'Mother of the Word Incarnate.' Call her 'Our Life, Our Sweetness, and Our Hope.' Call her 'Our Lady of Lourdes, Our Lady of Guadalupe, Our Lady of Fatima, Our Lady of Bataan.' Call her all the pet names men have fashioned for her. Call her simply 'Woman,' the pet name of her Son.

"How Jesus must love women, to give that name to Mary. And how He must love Mary to call her by that name!

"Pronounce it just as He does, please, I beg you. With Godly dignity, with reverence, and awe, and joy, and shy, sweet wonder. Give it the mystery and the magic and the music His lips give it. And the kindness, and the courtesy, and the love with which His voice endowed it.

"Say to her, 'O Woman, through whom all women rose from chattels, God must love you dearly to give you such great sorrow. This myrrh is far more rare and costly than the gift the Magi brought. Woman, a bitter drink, but from the hand of God. How blessed are you, Mary!'

"And say, 'He chastens most whom best He loves, and only One shall drink a bitterer drink than yours; and only One shall feel the full weight of His hand. You feel that hand about to crush your heart? It does but shape it to the image of His Own.'

"All this she knows, of course. But, being Woman, she must hear it spoken. Speak, then, for God, and say, 'I love you.' Speak, too, for me, and all her children. Say, 'We love you, Woman.' And say, 'We'll find your little Boy!' "

St. Ignatius gestures to his army, a host more numerous than the stars, and limps his swift way to the Temple. The saints all vanish from my sight, save Brother

André, who built a shrine to St. Joseph, not so long ago, on a hill in Montreal.

"Pray let me comfort Joseph," Brother André begs. "He feels himself responsible for the loss of Jesus, and nothing Mary says can soothe him."

"Bless me, and go."

St. Martin I keep with me, that I may cry his tears.

"Martin, if I were a little child, I think — crippled, and hurt, and lost, and crying — and I could throw myself before her knees and call her 'Mother' — be to her a son who needs her — I think that I could cozen her to pity. Such pity as would blast the numb chill desolation of her soul and make her weep afresh. Not these sleety tears of loss. But warm refreshing tears, gushing from her eyes like summer rain to sweeten earth, tears that would soften her sad heart so that it could not break."

"Ah, she would take you in her arms and hug you tightly. She would heal your hurts, and bless you, Blindman. But cozen? No."

"But, in many ways I am a little child, malformed by sin, hurt with her sorrow, and lost — aye, truly lost without her."

"Let us go find her."

God favors those He loves

The night is overlong. I blow it from me with a breath.

The day is long, and hot, and filled with heartbreak. I blow the hours from me, one by one, unable to endure them as does Mary.

We find her near the Temple steps at last, sitting on a bench with Joseph, Bernard and André standing guard beside them.

"O Blindman," Brother André greets me, "this is the saddest day inflicted on this earth. Look you, my Joseph's beard is bleached white with his grief. Tears have burned out his eyes. His voice is gone. His legs can carry him no further."

"And Mary barely breathes," says St. Bernard. "Sorrow hangs so heavily on her that she cannot move. She faints. Our valiant mother faints! She faints, revives, moans pitifully, and murmurs, 'Jesus.'

"See how the teeth of sorrow have gnawed her loveliness! Once when she fainted I saw her eyes. Shriveled beneath those swollen lids. And lifeless! And her sweet mouth — "

But our Lady's eyes are opening. Her head is lifting. And her arms.

She rises, and Joseph with her. She hurries up the stairs, and Joseph follows slowly.

Splendor of Sorrow

And now I hear the limping step of St. Ignatius, which they had heard before we did, and I see Him hurrying to Mary.

"We've found Him. St. Anthony found Him in the Temple, confounding all the doctors."

"God bless you," Mary answers. She does not move. She stands on the top stair, enchanted by a voice I cannot hear — a voice that pours her beauty back into her face, that floods her eyes with love and rapture and makes her weary body new — the musical voice of Jesus.

And Joseph stands at Mary's side. His face glows, and his beard shines in the setting sun. But there is no rebirth of strength in him. These last three days have sucked the marrow from his bones and swallowed his resilience. His end is not far off.

I cannot see my Lord. He is hidden from me by five saints I sent to find Him, five saints so spellbound by their Master's voice — and logic — they have forgotten all save Him — five holy Doctors of the church.

"Son, why have You done so to us? Behold, Your father and I have sought You sorrowing."[11]

---

[11] Luke 2:48.

The holy joy in her reproaches! Heart-break speaking in the tones of bliss. Bliss speaking with the tongue of woe.

How speedily joy flowers from the soil of sorrow!

"How is it that you sought me? Did you not know that I must be about my Father's business?"[12]

Ah, and sorrow blossoms quickly in the soil of joy.

"My Father's business." Words that will haunt her through the years. Wounds that will stay fresh, that will not scar.

Words of her little Boy — a Boy like other boys, living in a dream of manhood, knowing the irresistible human urge to prove Himself of age — as boys do who pull a razor down a satin cheek, wear pants too long and hats too big, read books beyond their years, and utter thoughts beyond their comprehension.

A Boy who has, like others of His age, leaped — in a human moment — across the long, slow-creeping years of adolescence — urged by divine impatience to begin His Father's work.

It is the Boy who speaks, but through the mouth of God — whom none may question or reproach.

[12] Luke 2:49.

"But, ah," says Martin, "the Man is gone, beneath His mother's eyes. And the Boy is back, somewhat confused, awakened from His dream of manhood."

I see Him now, His sun-bleached hair ashine against the blue of Mary, His arms about her, his lips uplifted for her kiss.

And I can see the heavenly joy of Mary, and read St. Joseph's mind.

"He must be tired after all this preaching; and I shall carry Him to bed!"

The Fourth Sorrow:
The Way of the Cross

~

Mary teaches you to
embrace the crosses
God sends you

My dear Lord approaches slowly.

Not through the brambles and the briers, to find me hurt and helpless, to heal and cleanse me, to take me lovingly in His arms and carry me back to the fold.

Not stealing quietly into my room to listen to my prayers.

Nor along the altar rail, the King of Glory, white and resplendent, restoring hopes as He passes, filling sad hearts with sweetness, giving Himself in a foretaste of Heaven.

No, He comes now, stooped and staggering beneath a Cross, along the road to Calvary.

And Mary, His mother, with a little band of saints around her, waits on a knoll beside the way, patient and mute and still. She is in black — black that looks warm and kind against her somber cheeks, against her blood-less hands.

Splendor of Sorrow

A while ago I saw my God in Pilate's hall, standing erect and kingly, in the purple robe by which men mocked His kingship, with the reed they gave Him for a scepter, with the crown of thorns set deliberately askew in ribald malice.

A while ago, as Pilate washed his hands, I saw men snatch the reed and lash my Lord across His pitying eyes. I saw them spit upon Him. I saw them take the purple rag from Him. It caught on the thorns, points sharper than the fangs of adders. A soldier yanked the circlet off His head, not caring how it raked and tore, not caring what bits of flesh and hair came with it.

I saw His back — an altar cloth, blackened and scorched and striped by fire, hacked by impious hands into a snarl of lace and ribbons, and smeared with a sticky wine, a holy red wine seeping from a broken chalice.

I saw them put His own clothes on Him, jamming the crown once more down hard to gouge His sacred flesh. I saw them kick Him, smash Him with their fists, pummel His whip-torn back, pelt Him with clubs and stones and filth and offal, and hustle Him, in drunken exultation, to the waiting Cross.

And I saw Him, although not clearly, outside the Praetorium, in the midst of a noisy rabble.

Mary teaches you to embrace the crosses

"I am the reed that struck You," I cried, "the bruised reed You did not break. I am the beloved who sold You. I am the judge who found You innocent — and condemned You."

The dust hid Him from me. My mouth was filled with it, and my nostrils. And I smelled the sweet new wood of the Cross, and the sweat of mules and men. And my ears were filled with blasphemies and curses.

"I have done this," I murmured, "and I shall do more. I shall strip You naked, Jesus. I shall drive great nails of iron through You. Through Your quivering, shuddering flesh I shall beat spikes. I shall hammer and bludgeon and pinion You to that Cross that weighs You down; fasten You hand and foot securely. And as Your fingers curl and writhe and dance with pain; as Your shocked blood scurries from the nails, and then returns, in panic, to the open wounds, as spasms of agony ripple through Your body, then I shall mock You, Jesus!

"O God, my Savior, for my sins, I pray You, turn me back into the dust from which Your Father made me. Strew me in this road before You. Let me be deep and cool and soft, to ease Your burned and blistered soles. Let me be mingled with the common dust, and be unknown, forgotten, lost. Lost in the dust beneath Your sacred feet!

"Yet, for the love I bear You, let me kiss the feet that spurn me. Let me absorb and hold the precious blood that drips upon me.

"And, in Your own time, lift me on the wings of all the winds and scatter me throughout the world, that I may bring the power and the glory and the fire and the love of You to all my fellow sinners!"

"Dust crying unto dust," a soft voice whispered. "But He has heard you, Blindman." St. Francis de Sales looked down upon me. "Aye, dust you are, and dust will be again. And you do absorb the precious blood each morning at Communion. Not only His blood, but His whole Body, His Soul, and His Divinity!

"Oh dust that wraps God in yourself, you will be lifted up on wings and spilled across the earth, in His good time. But on the wings of words, which are mightier than the wings of any winds that blow, which carry farther, and which cannot die."

"Patron of writers," I begged him, "give me an alms of tears, and lead me whither I may see Him best."

"You must be close to Mary, if you would see Him best," the saint replied.

And now I stand with Mary, outside the Genath Gate, and Jesus is coming toward us.

Mary teaches you to embrace the crosses

St. John, a tall gaunt stripling, sobs aloud; but our Lady keeps her silence.

She must be fifty now, or near it. Yet never was a woman of her age so lovely. Why are her cheeks still soft and young and fresh, her mouth still beautiful and tender? Why have her sorrows left no lasting mark upon her face? Is it because she lived so long, so intimately with Jesus, the essence and the source of beauty? Is it because her wounds are far too deep to show their scars?

She must have known great anguish when she lost St. Joseph — and when she said goodbye to Jesus, that day He started on His Father's business.

She must have borne long, heavy, crushing days without Him. She must, at times, have journeyed far in the hope of gazing at Him — and not found Him.

Yet, she seems but little older than when I saw her at the Presentation.

Straight she stands, resigned and patient. But a vein throbs madly in her temple, a signal whipping in a gale of sorrow, flashing a code not hard to read. Her bosom falls and rises with the tides of her emotions. And her hands, her dead-white screaming hands, the way she holds them, the way her knuckles stare at me — like wee white ghosts that whimper — her hands reveal more woe than even her pain-steeped eyes. There is such hurt in her that all the world is wounded.

And desperation pounds its fists in all my veins, desperation at my helplessness to aid her — and the sense of guilt that fills me.

"It is the will of God that she suffer," says St. Francis. "And her will, too. By suffering is the world redeemed. And you would dull her anguish with the anaesthesia of tears?"

"If I could, St. Francis."

"Tell me, when you saw the Savior, flogged and mocked and ridiculed and beaten — disfigured and distorted as He was — did you not thrill to see Him? Did you not feel a heavenly wonder seeping through you? Did you not see Infinite Grandeur, Infinite Rapture, Infinite Love? Did you not see Jesus?

"Thus will His mother see Him. With joy as well as sorrow. And who shall say which steel shall strike more keenly — the sword of sorrow or the rapier of joy?"

"The sword of love will cut most deeply," says St. Thomas Aquinas.

"Christ is her life, yet she wills that He must suffer, that He must die. For unless He suffer, and unless He die, how can we, her much loved children, live?

"Was ever woman placed in such a situation, that she must pray, that she must hope to see the death of Him she loves with all her heart — and must rejoice when He is dead — because of her love for those who slay Him?"

"Ah, she should hate us!"

"She cannot hate, since hate is sin, and she immaculate. She loves us. No human heart can hold such depths of love, save that shaped in her womb."

"Her love for Jesus and for us," exclaims St. John Chrysostom. "A two edged-sword! And, ah, how cruelly sharp its edges. But yet she welcomes it.

"In her own way, she, too, will suffer crucifixion for us. Behold our co-redemptress!"

"How wonderful we are," cries St. Augustine, "that God must die for us, and Mary suffer!

"Oh lavish, wasteful, infinite love of Jesus! It is not enough to give us all He has. He must add His mother's love to His.

"O Virgin-Mother, made immaculate by God, wooed by God, and filled with God, how wonderful we are — and how unworthy!"

Dust blazes now upon the road before us, and light gleams in its yellow swirling — the sun rays shattered and scattered by the Roman spears. And clamor grows, and furious confusion.

"He comes," our Lady says. Her voice is low and soft, stirring the heart in my constricted bosom.

The throbbing in her temples stills. Her hands are hidden. Her eyes are veiled by their long lashes. The tides in her have ebbed, and left her breathless.

The dust is nearer.

And now a man breaks through it, a soldier on a restless horse, the centurion, Longinus. He comes as from a fog. And men on mules come after him, and a soldier bearing an inscription: "Jesus of Nazareth, King of the Jews"; then squads of soldiers, and a host of shouting, cursing, snarling, spitting, lusting men.

And there is Jesus, bent almost double by the heavy beams. The crown of thorns, dull green and ugly brown, is plaited tight about His shining head, gashing it in a hundred places. His face is wet with tiny rills of blood, with perspiration, with the spittle of the mob, and with the divine love of sinners that wells from His half-blinded eyes.

Feebly He walks, despite the urging of the mob, who scarce can wait to see Him die.

He falls. Abruptly. He pitches forward, striking His head against the wood, driving the lances of the thorns deep into His skull, tearing His hands and feet on the jagged stones in the way and on the hard splinters of the Cross. And resin, oozing from the sun-scorched timber, drips like molten acid to smirch and sear Him.

A moment He lies there in the dust and grit, steam rising from His wet red back. They jerk His head up by the chin. They dig hard fingers into the hollows of His shoulders, and pull Him upward. They prod Him with the tips of spears and smack His soles with the flat of swords.

The Cross is on His shoulder once again, biting into it, crushing it, grinding it with every step He takes, churning it crimson raw. Again He stumbles onward toward us, His face streaked now with dust as well as tears and sweat and slime and blood — but still the King of Kings.

And now He sees His mother!

"O saints so rich in words," I plead, "preach to me of this look that burns in the eyes of Son and mother; this look of lightning that destroys them both yet does not kill them; tell me of the love that both consumes and strengthens them, the love they sacrifice for us."

But the saints are silent, more eloquent thus than ever they were in script or sermon.

Mary wavers with the shock. And Jesus falters.

That He should see Her thus, so dear, so beautiful, so wracked with grief and pity, so docile and resigned! That she should see Him so!

He stumbles. Men seize Him, hold Him fast. Longinus calls a halt, and singles out a black man from the crowd of onlookers near the mound.

"You there — what do they call you?"

"Simon."

"You are a Cyrenian?"

"Aye."

"This Man needs help. Take hold there. Quickly."

The man is unwilling. Why should he be implicated in this monstrous crime? But he must bow to Caesar. He lifts the heavy wood. And finds it light!

"How dear all black people must be to our Savior," says the great St. Albert, "and to our blessed mother. Of all the men on earth, but one is chosen to aid Christ in His Passion. This Simon of Cyrene. This kindly black man. Ah, well does Jesus know how hard a cross all black people carry, and will carry through the ages."

"To those He loves most," St. Jerome declares, "He gives the heaviest crosses. And those who love Him most, discover that the heaviest cross is lightest."

Mary teaches you to embrace the crosses

A woman bursts now through the ranks of soldiers, and wipes the face of Jesus with a veil her tears have moistened.

"Why did not Mary think of that?" I wonder. "Why did she make no slightest move to help Him?"

It is St. Benedict who answers.

"It was not written so in Heaven. Our Lady must not save Him from the least discomfort. He must bear all. And so must she.

"Our Lady is the living will of God. Veronica knows nothing of this will. She knows but love — and bravery, the child of love — and pity, love's twin sister. And for her love, see what a priceless gift she holds, stamped on her veil!"

My Lord has gone; but Mary's eyes yet watch the road before us. There is still traffic there, cursing and shouting men, soldiers, idlers, two thieves who carry crosses.

"They, too, John?" our Lady asks.

"They, too," the beloved apostle answers. "They will die with Him, Mother."

Tears gather slowly on the black lace of our Lady's lashes, slowly acquire shape and luster, and slowly fall, as beads fall through the fingers of a nun — a rosary of tears, shed not for Jesus but for sinners.

"Holy Mary, Mother of God," the words rip out of me unconsciously, "pray for us sinners now and at the hour of our death."

"Amen," St. Viator adds. "And pray especially for these, your doomed and recreant children."

"St. Viator, sing," I shout. "Sing, all you holy saints. Sing for the wonder of these tears. Sing *Alleluia* 'til the heavens echo, and all the angels answer *Alleluia!*"

The traffic halts again. I look toward Calvary to see the reason.

For the second time my Lord has fallen. And a fierce wild grief enrages me, so that I forget our Lady's tears, the saints, the thieves, and everything and everyone but Jesus.

"This is enough," I think, "and I must end it. Let all the world be damned, He shall not die if I can save Him."

But even as I hug this thought I thrust it from me, and fall in penitence at my Lady's feet. It was my will that spawned this blasphemy. Not His. Not Mary's.

"You love Him, Blindman?"

My Lady's voice is gentle. And, oh, her breath is sweet!

"Yes, Mother. Yes, I love Him. With all my crazy heart I love Him; with all my sinful soul. More and more each day, I love Him, Mother. 'More than yesterday; less than tomorrow!' "

"Rise, then," she bids me, "Come stand with me beneath His Cross, and see how He loves you!"

The Fifth Sorrow:
The Crucifixion

⁀

Christ takes all
your sorrows on Himself

The Lamb of God at last has reached the altar.

"*Et introibo ad altare Dei.*"[13] Now let the Mass begin.

The Cross is taken from Him and lowered to the ground. Men surround Him, jostling, pushing, spitting, impatient for the kill. Teeth gleam. Lips foam. Saliva drools into unkempt beards. Eyes are swollen and inflamed with lust and malice. Dirty hands are raised in anger. And voices shrill with passion clamor —

"Crucify Him! Crucify Him!"

Above them shimmers the iridescent dust, dancing as heat waves dance.

St. John is clutching his hair and rocking his head in helpless woe. The Magdalen is on her knees, her rose-gold tresses hiding her face. Her fists beat hard against the earth.

[13] "And I will go to the altar of God."

Splendor of Sorrow

Our Lady stands between the two, serene and straight and beautiful. And stricken. In splendid contrast against the ugliness, the shame, the tumult, and the violence, she stands. In regal resignation.

Dry gusts of horror have blown away her tears, but have not dried the pity in her eyes, pity for her children and her Child. The sun is shining on her face, making a halo of the dust about her, highlighting her firm chin and wide, white forehead.

She makes no move to help this dearest One of all her children, the only One of all her brood she cannot, must not, succor. Her soft lips move in prayer, but not to comfort Him. They beg forgiveness for all who torture Him. They ask His love for those who love Him not, for those who hate Him. Her hands are joined in solemn supplication, mute advocates invoking mercy for the merciless and pity for the cruel.

Roughly, a soldier wrests from the holy head the crown of thorns. It claws the Savior spitefully as it leaves, exacting priceless treasure.

And they strip Him.

The seamless robe, saturated with His blood, baked by the sun and ground by the heaviness of the Cross into His flesh, has become one with the fabric of His back, that wondrous satin woven in the womb of Mary by the love of the Holy Spirit. It will not be parted from Him save through force.

Strong hands tug at the stubborn wool and rip it free. But, ah, a hundred tiny patches of His skin adhere to it.

Jesus reels with the matchless pain.

A quick indrawn breath — more frightful to hear than any scream — interrupts His mother's prayer. The red ebbs from her lips. Her shoulders quiver. And she is still again.

Naked and shamed, Divine Love stands before His creatures, to be laughed at, to be mocked.

"A naked king," they shout. "A naked God. A man like any other man. Crucify Him! Crucify Him!"

And one demands, "Give Him His crown. Even on His deathbed, a king should wear His crown."

He lies upon the Cross, without protest, without resistance. His raw back is pressed against rough wood and scalding resin. His arms are outstretched, waiting for the nails; His feet are held by soldiers; His head rests on His thorns.

The hammers rise and fall, rise and fall, rise and fall.

Slowly they rise, gleaming for a moment in the sun. Swiftly they fall. Iron crashes against iron, against the surface of the pine, against the softness of His hands and feet. The sounds grate against my teeth and set them to an exquisite aching.

Mary's eyes are frightened and dark and swollen. Her dry lips tremble. Her hands are at her sides, and cupped as His are cupped against the agony of the nails. White tulips, they seem, held thus against the deep black of her dress. White tulips shaking in a cruel wind.

The Cross is raised, on the shoulders of men, and brought to the edge of the hole dug for it.

I fall on my knees, and bow my head, and beat my breast.

There is a hush, such as comes before the Elevation in the Mass, when the last echoes of the great organ cease reverberating, and no one stirs.

The Cross is dropped. Suddenly. Expertly. Vertically. It is dropped with a jolt that all but tears His hands loose from the wood; with a shock that throws His head forward, then sharply back against the beam, so that the thorns cut deep; with a jar that plunges Him, helpless, into a raging flood of pain.

Men hold it steadily in place, while others shovel dirt into the pit, and stamp it tightly down.

And He hangs there, dancing a ghastly dance!

Christ takes all your sorrows on Himself

The wounds have lengthened in His palms. His face is as white as Our Lady's hands. It is so white that the blood and the tears and the bruises and the spittle and the dirt stand out in hideous relief against His flesh.

"Father, forgive them," He whispers, "for they know not what they do."[14]

Fear racks me. I cover my face, even as the Magdalen has done. And I mutter to the dust beneath me, "But I knew, Lord Jesus. Only too well I knew. *Mea culpa. Mea culpa. Mea culpa.* Lamb of God, have mercy on me!"

His mother stands close to Him, her head upraised to drink the bitter chalice offered, her arms stretched out and reaching upward.

A woman cheated of her Child, and jealous of the tree that holds Him. A priestess of the old rite, sacrificing, with the knife of her will, the snow-white Lamb she bore; a priestess of the new, saying, in the chapel of her body, on the altar of her heart, the world's first Mass.

Saying it with Him. Offering His body and His blood to the Father, as humbly and as eagerly and as reverently as He does Himself. In perfect adoration. In thanksgiving for all the blessings showered on mankind. In reparation

[14] Luke 23:34.

for our sins. And in petition for all sinners, the living and the dead.

I kiss the hem of her mantle ere I dare lift my head.

The sun has fled in fear and loathing from the earth. The moon has drawn her curtains tight. And all the stars have closed their eyes.

Never, since God said, "Let there be light," has there been such darkness on the earth. Yet, I with my eyes that can see nothing, see Him perfectly, outlined sharply against the night, a white shape that might be an angel, wings spread, gliding toward me. I see Him, and I no longer fear.

Voices bid Him come down from the Cross if He be truly God. Even the thieves, dying on either side of Him, assail Him.

And lo, again I see, and feel, the benediction of our Lady's tears.

St. Joseph stands close to her, a young and beautiful and strong St. Joseph, whose right hand pats her shoulder, whose voice keeps saying, "My dear, my very dear."

And St. Joachim is with her. And St. Ann. And St. John Bosco. And so many others, sinners and saints, I cannot name them all. But there is no comfort in them.

Don Bosco kneels beside me.

"At His death, as at His birth," he says, "those who love Him bring Him gifts. Mary gives Him the myrrh in her heart, St. John the incense of his courage, and the Magdalen the priceless gold of sorrow. What do you bring Him, Blindman?"

"Only the tears I cannot shed."

"Take mine, and welcome. You envy the Magdalen?"

"I always have. I always shall."

"Envy her not, my son. The precious ointment Christ pours out on her, He pours into your body at Communion."

"It is not this I envy her, dear saint, but the wealth of contrition she places at His bleeding feet."

"Ah, that! I, too, have envied her that gift. But only great sinners can amass such store of treasure. Great sinners, and great lovers."

Christ looks upon His mother, and speaks to her for the last time, using the old pet name "Woman, behold your son." He looks at John. "Behold your mother!"[15]

"In the garden of Eden," Don Bosco says, "there was a tree, the fruit of which was forbidden under pain of death. Our first parents ate that fruit, Blindman, and death came to the world.

[15] John 19:26-27.

"Look now upon the tree in this garden of redemption, and upon the Fruit that hangs thereon. This Fruit we are commanded to eat, that we may live. The Fruit of the Cross. The Fruit of Mary's womb.

"We eat of this Fruit, and it is part of us. This blood pouring from Him in rivers of love — O my Jesus, how You squander it upon us! — we drink for the sustenance of our souls. His blood, and Mary's.

"This body — only last night He willed it to us — is flesh of Mary's flesh, bone of her bone. It dies that it may never die, that it may nourish men until the world crumble and is lost.

"We are parts of the Mystical Body of Christ. He is the head. We are the members, the humble cells. We are parts of the mystical body of Mary's Son. Therefore — don't you see? — we are the children of His mother — as truly as is St. John.

"Death came to us from Eve. Life comes to us from Mary. From Mary and the Holy Spirit. Through them did Jesus come to us. Through them, let us go to Jesus. And through Jesus to the Father."

"And let us," I answer, "go to Mary, through you, Don Bosco, and all the other saints, who love her, whom she loves, whom she cannot deny."

Christ takes all your sorrows on Himself

The beloved apostle wipes his eyes and kisses our Lady's hand.

"Mother," he says, "I am a most unworthy son."

He kneels at her feet, and Mary strokes his hair with the fingers he has kissed. But she is looking not at him, nor at Jesus, but at the young thief on the cross.

A light shines through the dark. It is not the flame of a torch held high by a curious soldier. It is not a flash of lightning. It is a light, a glory, an unearthly beauty, radiating from the face of Jesus and illuminating the features of the thief.

I see the face of a boy, weary and wondering and lost, and in frightful pain; a face running with blood and tears and sweat.

His arms and legs are fastened to the cross with ropes that have cut deep into his flesh and raised white ridges. His ribs have almost burst their scabby prison. His undernourished belly beats in frantic rhythm against the bars of death. He groans in pain and curses in despair.

His eyes are puzzled, at first, meeting the gaze of Jesus. They flash defiance, then. Then remorse, and courage; and suddenly they light with love. And he is beautiful.

"The face of a sinner," says Don Bosco, "looking for the first time on the loving face of God."

Splendor of Sorrow

Ah, hear the chorus of angels chanting, "*Gloria in Excelsis Deo.*" See the gates of Heaven swinging wide to welcome a thief and murderer, a sinner dying, through the grace of God, a saint — the first man in all the generations of the earth for whom those gates have opened.

Tears streak, skipping joyously, down the face of my Lord, tears that sparkle like a chain of brilliants. He turns to the other thief and waits for him to speak. But this man, stubborn and proud and vengeful, curses and reviles Him.

"You, too, could have found rest against my Sacred Heart," the eyes of Jesus seem to say. "You, too, could be with me tonight in Paradise — for one word, one thought. But you would not. You would not!"

His tears do not sparkle now, nor do they dance.

It is dark again, so dark I barely see Him. And He cries, "My God, my God, why have You forsaken me?"[16]

"It is near the end," Don Bosco tells me. "His body has taken all the punishment it can endure. It is His spirit that suffers now.

"O man whose eyes see so clearly through plaster and wood and brick, and night, and leagues of years, you

[16] Matt. 27:46.

90

cannot even dimly envisage the supreme agony that afflicts His soul!

"This is the most frightful moment in all eternity, the most glorious, and the most mysterious. God is forsaken by God! God endures what is to God the unendurable, the impossible. God, who is Heaven, allows Himself to suffer Hell — for love of us!

"O almighty God of love! O almighty love of God!

"The damned suffer because they have never seen the Father, and never will. Because they have never loved Him. Because they are forsaken by Him.

"Jesus alone knows the Father in all His glory. Jesus alone loves Him as He must be loved. Far worse than the damned in the lowest pit of Hell does He suffer who has known God through all eternity, who has loved God with a divine love, who is God, who is by God given into the hands of men!

"How tame, how childish, how utterly senseless our attempts to hurt Him, compared with this incomprehensible torture He inflicts upon Himself! What greater proof of love can He show us than in thus allowing the breath of Hell to scorch His sinless soul?

"You saw Him whipped and beaten. You saw Him deviled with a hundred piercing thorns. You saw Him carrying His heavy Cross. You saw Him transfixed with His mother's suffering look. You saw Him flayed when they stripped Him naked. You saw Him nailed to the Cross. You saw Him deluged with pain when they dropped the Cross into its hole.

"Yet you heard no word, no murmur from His lips.

"But now, this Man who stilled the waves and the winds with a gesture of His hand, who cleansed the lepers, who gave sight to the blind and quickened the dead, this Man who is Almighty God, cries out like a little child against this moment.

"Yet He endures it, willingly, for us.

"O Blindman, this is the greatest love story ever told. The love of Jesus Christ for sinners. The love of God for man!"

The moment passes. My blessed Lord is conscious again of His torn and dying body. He thirsts. And men laugh. And lift vinegar to His parched and burning lips.

Vinegar, my Savior, from us You love so much!

And now it is consummated.

Ite Missa Est. The Mass is ended. Go.

He has finished His Father's work. He has redeemed the world. He has given us His body and His blood. He has offered Himself in sacrifice for us. He has established

His church on earth. He has opened Heaven. He has done all things appointed Him to do.

Go, and live the Mass.

He is ready to die, to rush into the waiting arms of His Father. He calls out in a loud voice, an exultant voice, a voice that still peals gloriously through Heaven and earth.

"Father, into Your hands I commend my spirit."[17]

Mountains bow to the dying God. Hills crumble. The hard ground surges like the sea. Lightnings crack the black-glazed sky and flick the craven soil. A tidal wave of thunder rolls above me, and fingertips of nausea drum upon my brain.

Tombs belch forth the unwrapped dead. And they march by me, with the smell of charnel spices strong upon them, proclaiming through their lipless mouths that life is born of death.

Panic screams in every breast, "This was the Son of God!" And those who mocked and jeered a little time ago run where they may, stumbling and falling, panting, in terror of their lives.

The Temple veil is rent from top to bottom; and the Holy of Holies is exposed to all the people.

[17] Luke 23:46.

"And thus," Don Bosco assures me, "shall it be henceforward. Forever and forever the Holy of Holies shall be accessible to all who love the Lord, to all His children who need comfort, or advice, or surcease of pain. Forever and forever Jesus Christ will abide among us, awaiting our visits, our tears, our prayers.

"Jesus is dead upon the Cross. Jesus lives forever on the earth."

Our Lady stands in her place, unmoving. But her hands are no longer cupped like tulips at her side. She holds them now against her heart, clenched as though they held the pommel of a sword — a sword she would not draw from its sweet scabbard, if she could — the sword of our salvation.

"Who can comfort her, Don Bosco?"

"Look at her closely, Blindman," the saint advises.

Her eyes are still aglow with tears; but a look shines through them that bewilders me. I have seen that look in the eyes of other women who have given sons to God, or king, or country. Yet never, until this second, did I see it in our Lady.

Long I stand there at the foot of the Cross, on the pitching earth, among rocks that explode into powder, in dust that stings, in the midst of the walking dead, in the pandemonium of the living, in the lightnings and the thunder, in the fury of the dark.

Long I stand, gazing on that lovely, weeping, glorious, uplifted face of Mary and the light that blazes in her eyes — the light of pride in her Son. Pride that is stronger than woe. Pride in His love for men, in His divine sacrifice, in His shameful death!

She needs no human consolation in that pride.

Pride? Aye, and more than pride.

Pride, and a holy triumph!

The Sixth Sorrow:
Jesus is taken down from the Cross

*Mary longs to
draw you close to Christ*

The fury of the lightning dies. The thunder scampers off with surly growls. The earth is steadied. The dead return to rest. The sun has reappeared, and the blinded night begins again to see.

Behold the Source of life hanging lifeless on a barren hill, and the shadow of His Cross stretching east and west and north and south across the world. Behold the sunlight shining through the dust, draping the nakedness of God in its own glory! Behold the golden splendor in our Lady's eyes!

Once, ere God gave me the gift of blindness, I watched an eclipse of the sun. Through smoke-stained glass I saw the silver moon serenely skimming through the azure sky until it came 'twixt sun and earth. Then it turned black and flat. It moved with menace across the sun's bright face, casting a pall on earth, frightening animals and men.

Splendor of Sorrow

The sun shrank as the black vampire sucked its blood, became a waning crescent of itself, and then a dwindling splinter. Yet, before its light was gone, it sowed the world with images of itself, which gleamed like silver sequins on a dancer's dress.

On every blade of grass about my feet, on every leaf of every tree, on every stem and every petal of every flower, upon my hands and on my garments, I saw the miniatures of the dying sun, the waning crescents and the dwindling splinters.

Now, in the eclipse of the Crucifixion, I view this miracle again; for here, wedged tight between horizon and horizon, are all the saints of Heaven, each with a crucifix held high as though it were a torch to light the way. And on each image of the Master, even those in the deepest shadow, the wonder of the sunshine gleams.

"There is a glory in His death that cannot die," I hear myself exclaiming, "a glory distributed to all who love Him. But why does it blaze so joyously in the eyes of His mother — who must be overwhelmed with woe and horror?"

St. Alphonsus Liguori puts the crucifix to his lips before he answers. He kisses face and feet and heart and hands. He holds the image pressed against his breast. He speaks in a lover's voice.

"Woe and horror you will never know consume her. Her body scarcely can live beneath its weight of sorrow. Yet, when He died, her spirit leaped with ecstasy as, long ago, her heart leaped when her Babe first stirred within her.

"That joy sustains her, Blindman, in her death-sharp anguish — joy that He has made complete the work of our redemption, joy that He has soared in triumph back to Heaven and opened it for all her children!

"How beautiful she is, Our Lady of Compassion! How dear! How utterly unselfish! How filled with joy for Him — and us — in the depths of her own agony and desolation!"

Longinus, the centurion, stands at the foot of the Cross, lance lifted, poised, and sparkling in the sun.

"Blindman, you have seen eternity's most frightful and mysterious moment," whispers St. Alphonsus. "Witness now its most beautiful and precious."

Longinus thrusts his weapon quickly, cleanly, deeply, into the heart of Jesus, then draws it from the wound.

Bright blood gushes from our Savior's side. And water.

"The wine and water of the Mass," I gasp.

"The sacraments of Communion and Baptism," the saint responds. "The blood and tears of the Sacred Heart of Jesus!"

He bows his head.

"The heart of God is opened to the hearts of men. And from this moment it shall never fail to pour out blood and tears to win our love, so long as there are blood and tears in men."

"Blood, the rubies of our redemption," the lyric nun, St. Margaret Mary, cries. "And tears, the riches of His pity for our weaknesses, our stubbornness, our wicked pride, our coldness to His love!

"O blessed lance, how sweetly hast thou dug for us a path to the Sacred Heart; a path for our hopes, our needs, our thanks, our love, to travel; a channel from the very core of love into every heart that beats!"

Stupendous thoughts have crushed her outcry to the faintest of faint whispers; and there is a stirring in the ranks of the blessed that shuts it from my ears.

Long lines of saints are forming, moving in procession past the Cross, saints in the black robe of the Jesuit, in the brown garb of St. Francis, in the uniforms of fighting men, in the attire of civilians.

Mary longs to draw you close to Christ

The flames of candles flicker. Smoking censers swing, spilling clouds of incense on the sun-clad body. And in a chorus that out-thunders thunder and rings like all the glad bells caroling through time, the happy dead take up St. Margaret Mary's cry of adoration.

"O blessed lance that kissed the heart of Jesus and made it forever and forever ours!

"O cleansing, consoling, healing blood: O life-giving water pouring from the body of Our Lord!

"O eternal fountain of love bubbling from the bosom of God the Son!

"O never-ending stream of the power and the wisdom and the purification of God the Holy Spirit!

"O everlasting and abundant well of the mercy of God the Father!"

The rays of the sinking sun are focused on the water welling from the side of Jesus, and on the mist in Mary's eyes. I look at them through the water and the mist and see a rainbow, God's covenant of mercy, arched on the gold and red and purple sky above the Cross.

And abruptly it is night. The moon and the vesper star have risen in the East. Vigil lights are burning overhead. The chorus of the saints is stilled. The water and the wine have ceased to flow.

Splendor of Sorrow

Our Lady stands unmoving in her place, face uplifted in love and agony and triumph, her hands upon her heart, until St. John and Nicodemus climb ladders into the little stars, and Joseph of Arimathea takes his stand below.

Swiftly the three men work to draw the nails, which have been bent and twisted and hammered into the wood, that they might better hold. Swiftly and gently — careful to do no hurt to this sweet corpse which has been hurt so much.

John brings the body down, one hand holding the head of Jesus firmly against his breast.

"Last night," St. Gertrude says, "at the last supper, man listened to the beating heart of God. Tonight God hears the beating heart of man."

Tenderly John places the body in our Lady's arms. She clutches Him greedily, with a holy hunger. The tears she would not shed while He could see her, fall now unrestrained upon the tapestry of blood and slime and sweat and tears and dirt and death that hides the beauty of His face.

Her shoulders flutter, like the wings of a dove impaled and dying. And sobs break like waves in the sea of sorrow in her breast.

"Jesus, Jesus, Jesus, O my Son!"

Drab skeins of grief and shame are knotted in my heart; and for relief I whisper to her, "It was not the Jews who killed Him, Mother; it was not the Romans; it was all of us. It was I. Weep for us, Mother. Weep especially for me, who cannot weep."

The Magdalen lifts her swollen and distorted face. "And weep for me." Her voice is low and husky, devoid of vehemence or strength. "These ugly wounds! Mother, I made these ugly wounds in Him."

Our Lady rocks her Son as though he were again a child in need of sleep. She raises one of His cold hands to her cheek, warming and wetting it, recalling how once it dug into her breasts, played with her hair, and patted her young face.

"This beautiful body!" the Magdalen mourns. "These hands that were so quick to help, to comfort, and to heal. These feet that traveled earth and water and never tired in their quest for His lost sheep. This heart that so loved sinners. Mother, it was my sins that made these ugly wounds!"

"Ugly? Nay, never was such beauty stamped in human flesh."

It is St. Philip Benizi speaking. The seven holy founders of the Servants of Mary are with him, and St.

Peregrine, and St. Juliana, who died with the sacred Wafer melting into her heart. Near them are St. Dominic, and St. Catherine of Siena. And back of them, standing as close as corn stalks in a rustling field, are the ranks of Dominicans and Servites, in black habits, and in spotless white; the souls devoted to our Lady's rosaries.

"This is the new Garden of Eden, this body of our Lord," St. Philip says, "a paradise fashioned by lash and lance and nail and thorn for the happiness of all God's children.

"These are five roses, these red wounds. And see the little buds about His head! Centuries will pass, but these blooms will still be fresh, and fragrant. Roses. A Lover's gift. A garden of roses for the delight of His beloved!"

"Red flames," St. Dominic describes them. "Flames to set the world afire with love, to burn out sin, to comfort the cold and the weary and the sick, to light each life, and guide each soul to Heaven."

"They are mouths," St. Catherine asserts, "that sinners may kiss who dare not kiss His lips; mouths forever waiting for the lips of sinners."

"Mouths," St. Juliana echoes, "that eloquently speak of love, that hunger and thirst inordinately for love, most generous mouths eternally blessing men."

"Roses and flames and mouths," St. Peregrine reflects. "Aye, that is so. Roses to be watered with our tears, flames to hearten us, mouths to plead for us, mouths of honey waiting for our salty kisses. Yet, it seems to me, they are gems too, these sacred wounds, gems more precious than all the world, and all the souls they purchased."

Our Lady, lost in her own thoughts, has heard no word the saints have uttered. Her head is bent. Her lips are pressed against her Son's torn forehead, pouring out words between her kisses.

"My soul magnifies the Lord. And my spirit has rejoiced in God, my Savior. Yet do I weep for You, my Son, the Son of God Almighty, because I am a woman and Your mother.

"I weep because You are in my arms and take no warmth or comfort from me; because I speak to You and hear no loving answer on Your lips; because I look upon Your face and it returns no look of any kind to me. I weep that You are dead and turned to mortal clay. I weep for all the suffering You have endured and all the sins for which You suffered."

Women have fetched water for her, and soft cloths.

"See, Jesus," she murmurs, "here is water for You. Now that Your mortal thirst has ended, here is cold, pure water. Yet there is a divine thirst in You, even in this, Your lifeless body, which never can be slaked with water."

The moon halts in its course across the sky, to give her light; and the stars swoop down, as once before they swooped above a crib in Bethlehem. And Mary wipes the face of Jesus and bathes His body.

"It was for souls You thirsted on the Cross. And now. And always. The souls of those You gave me for my guidance; for my prayers, my love, my teaching, my protection.

" 'I thirst,' I heard You cry. And I gave You, through Your own grace, all the drink I could pour through Your lips. The tears of John and Mary Magdalen, the dying soul of the good thief hanging close to You, and my own pain and love and pity. And my own vow to bring souls to Your burning lips through all the centuries You shall thirst.

"He that is mighty has done great things to me, and holy is His name. He has exalted me above all women, and given all souls into my tending.

"Behold, henceforth all generations shall call me blessed; for they shall come to You through me, bearing the water of souls to quench Your holy thirst.

"Yet always, until the last of my children perish, shall You taste the gall and vinegar of sin. And always, and always, O my Jesus, shall You burn with thirst, the insatiable thirst of God!"

Her fingers caress the wound made by the lance, and linger there in blessing.

"Here was cold, pure water, too, dear Son, dear God, a torrent rushing from Your Sacred Heart to baptize all the world in the name of the Father, Son, and Holy Spirit, and make it Christian."

The word arouses her, shakes her, starts her tears afresh.

"O Jesus, by the love You owe me who bore You, who suckled You, who loved and adored You all Your life, let it be truly Christian!"

Her hands grip the wet cloth tightly. Water gushes from it like her tears. And my heart is squeezed as tightly as her cloth.

"This shaft she cannot bear, St. Dominic," I whisper, "this sword of revelation. She knows now that men will curse Him through the ages. She knows the name of Christian will be mocked and hated, that those who flaunt it proudly will make it a synonym for hypocrite and Pharisee and monster, a cloak for all the foulest sins man can commit, a symbol of injustice, persecution, murder, greed, and conquest.

"A little while ago she watched Him die; and yet her eyes were lit with triumph. There was a joy in her! But now, when she knows that He has died in vain — "

St. Dominic's right hand is placed against my lips.

"Do not blaspheme, my son," he warns me. "You do not know how precious is a soul. If He had come on earth and lived and died for the redemption of one soul, He had not lived, He had not suffered, He had not died in vain!

"One soul!

"His suffering and His death bought all the souls created by His Father. Yet if only one were delivered into His waiting arms — I do not say Christ would be content. Ah, no. But, so infinite is His love for souls, He would not find the price He paid for all too great to pay for one.

"Your soul is His, my son. It is as precious to God as the price He paid for it — the death of His Own Son! If it be lost — alas, it is yourself, then, who must pay for it in never-ending suffering and death. And your neighbor's soul is equally dear.

"Our Lady weeps, I grant you, because souls will be lost, will be forever damned. But most bitterly she weeps for Christians who will not live as Christians, though, through God's mercy and her prayers, they may die Christian deaths."

"Then does she weep for me," I cannot help confessing, "for I am the most un-Christian Christian of her sons."

"Then let us pray," and the saint's hands touch his beads.

It is a signal to all the Dominicans and Servites. They kneel in rows. In white rows, and in black. And each recites the rosary in silence, the five decades of the Dominicans, the seven septades of the Servites.

Our Lady rises, turns. She joins her hands and listens, then spreads them out as though to strew her blessings on the world.

"Observe, Blindman," St. Dominic takes time to whisper, "even in the profoundest depths of her sorrow, Our Lady gives her whole attention to her children's prayer.

"Her whole attention, and her whole sweet heart!"

The Seventh Sorrow:
Jesus is laid in the tomb

⁓

Christ brings
new life from the tomb

The night breathes like a woman spent with tragedy and sick for the kiss of sleep. A mist of tears has draped the moon and filmed the blazing eyes of stars. A wind weeps in the palm trees around and about Jerusalem, licks at an empty Cross, and hurries, whimpering, away from Israel.

And terror pulses through the earth.

The singing saints who chanted benedictions as the water and the wine poured from the Sacred Heart, the saints who scattered fragrant *Aves* on the corpse, as Mary bathed it, all these have gone, save one, the Blessed Mother Cabrini, who stays to comfort me.

John the beloved, and Joseph of Arimathea, and Mary Magdalen, and Mary of Cleophas have drawn aside to talk in whispers with Nicodemus, who has come in panting haste from the house of Caiphas, the high priest. And our Lady is left, for the moment, alone with her dead Son.

Splendor of Sorrow

The body lies on a white cerecloth, a body whiter than the cloth it graces. The taste of bread and wine is in my mouth as I gaze upon it; and in my nostrils is the smell of blood and resin.

The Virgin Mother, adjusting the cloth about Him, strokes His flesh with her exquisite fingers, anoints it with the chrism of her love and adoration, and consecrates it with her tears.

"See, Jesus, God and Child," she murmurs, "Your mother wraps You again in swaddling clothes."

Her tears wink like sparks of heavenly fire in the spectral light of the stars and the inconstant flare of torches.

"The shepherds are not here; but they will come. I promise. The wise men dally, but Your star will lead them hither through all the years to follow. The angels sing not; but they shall.

"Peace on earth? My Jesus, You have found it!

"You have found Joseph too, whom You loved so dearly — as he loved You. And holy Simeon who held You in his arms and begged for death that he might never know a lesser joy. And all the souls in Limbo hungering for You since the dawn of time.

"Give them the bliss Your death has filched from me. Make them as happy, Jesus, as I am sad."

Christ brings new life from the tomb

She draws the covering slowly over cheek and mouth and nose and brow and shining hair. Against her will. Shutting the face of God inexorably, bravely, sacrificially from her sight.

"Our Lady suffers as cruel a death as Jesus on the Cross," the kneeling nun reminds me. "The death of caring for Him, tending Him, watching Him, touching Him, waiting for the sound of His steps and the musical magic of His voice.

"Every impulse in her shrieks with outrage at this obliteration of the holy face, pleads for one more little glance, one final look. But she denies herself — that we may, the more surely, gaze forever on its beauty."

John comes to our Lady now, perturbed and hesitant.

"Mother, we must make haste. The sun is long since down. The Holy Day has overtaken us. It is the Sabbath, Mother."

"No, no," the Virgin answers, springing up. "It is not so."

She trembles, who did not quiver at the torture of her Son. Fright pulls at her lips, jerks at her nostrils, sucks the blood from her cheeks and the breath from her throat, and hammers at her temples. Fright magnifies her eyes, and moves her hands like puppets.

Splendor of Sorrow

"There is talk among the people," the venerable Nicodemus supplements St. John. "Some say we must entomb Him — that it is allowable because of the emergency — but we must do it quickly. Some say that, although the night has come, it is not yet the hour appointed for it and, therefore, not the Sabbath.

"But those who hate Him most maintain the Sabbath bides from nightfall unto nightfall, no matter when the darkness may descend. All nature was upset, they do admit — these Pharisees. Yet are they sly, and bent on doing further evil to Him now, although He be dead, and opening fresh wounds in those who love Him.

"They say, these children of iniquity, God was enraged at Pilate's jest, the inscription he had nailed upon the Cross, proclaiming the Messiah king of all the Jews — and that in His august anger He took away the sun and brought the Sabbath early. They say He acted so to punish Christ for blasphemy and treason — intending that His body should lie here unburied, to feed the ravens and the vultures! And now the high priest ponders fitting punishment for those who move the body!"

"We cannot leave Him here," the Magdalen exclaims. "And if we must, then I shall keep the Sabbath at His feet!"

"Peace," our Lady quiets her. " 'The Sabbath was made for man,' He said, 'not man for the Sabbath.' Is He not Lord of the Sabbath?"[18]

She kneels, serene again, and lifts to the skies a small handful of dust.

"We cannot see the sun," she whispers.

"In this same voice," the nun confides, "at a marriage feast in Cana, she said, 'They have no wine.' "[19]

I smell the dust that dribbles through her fingers. More sharply than the oil that lights the torches. More acutely than the pine that looms above me. I smell it and I feel it, and I watch it spread about me like the night.

It chokes. It blurs the vision of my blinded eyes. It coats my tongue. It stings my cheeks.

The rising wind is driving it through all my clothes. I struggle to my feet that I may flee. But I am powerless to move against the wind — a wind that cleanses me!

The smell of dust is gone. My lips are sweet. My tongue is moist. The particles of grit no longer rain upon my face. My eyes see clearly; and the panic that imperiled me is transformed into awe.

[18] Cf. Mark 2:27-28.
[19] John 2:3.

Splendor of Sorrow

A cloud of dirt and dust and grime and sand and mist is whirling, swirling, circling, rising, blowing up to Heaven — a curtain lifted in the theater of God, to show the westering sun still riding through the day!

Silver and gold and rose and mauve and grey gleam on us from the edges of white clouds. Crimson and orange and purple and wistaria and violet streak through the blue beneath. And there is the fire of the sun itself, fending off the Sabbath day to please its Virgin Queen.

Slowly now, the burial procession spills downhill — the last drop of Infinite Love to seep from the upset chalice and trickle from the altar of the Cross.

John and Joseph and Nicodemus carry the white-swathed body. Mary of Magdala, her torch extinguished, walks at the head of the mourners, while our Lady marches behind with Mary of Cleophas.

"A woman notorious throughout the world, why is it she who leads the Savior to His tomb?"

The words are but a thought, unformed, and not expressed. Yet the nun who guides my footsteps answers them. She speaks in a tongue I love, as men speak it in Chicago and New York, and towns and villages we both know well.

"It is a saint who leads the way, poor sinner," she rebukes me. "To the sepulcher — and to the Resurrection! She has that privilege because she bears Him in her heart. Because He loves her."

"He loves us all."

"But her especially. It was to her, and her alone, He wrote the letter."

"Our Savior wrote a letter?"

"His one love letter.

"Oh, God writes love letters to us all. We read them in the stars, in flowers, in trees, in lakes, in shells picked up beside the ebbing seas, in everything His love has given us. But the Son of God, 'bowing Himself down, wrote with His finger on the ground' a message meant entirely for Mary."

"What did He write?"

"She had been taken in her sin, and shamed by men who thought to stone her. She stood before her Lord, that He might judge and sentence her. He would not shame her. He stooped that she might not see His eyes. God is ever kind. And then He wrote."

"Wrote what?"

"Wrote all that ever filled His heart, His voice, His eyes, wrote all that ever motivated Him, or stirred Him, or led Him to the slaughter; wrote it in one word there on the ground.

"The one word — *Love!*

"It is love that leads Christ to His burial, Blindman, as it led Him through His life. It is love that leads the way to resurrection. Death and resurrection! Were He not human, He would not have died, would not be buried. And were He not divine, He could not rise again. Man he was, and so, loved God. God He is, and so, loves man.

"Love — love that burns and glows and sings and suffers, love that runs like a joyous dog to greet its master; love that finds no day too long, no night too dark, no task too hard, no ache too painful to endure for love — that love is symbolized in Mary Magdalen. See how it lights her eyes — her eyes made sweet by bitter tears. See how it sparkles in her hair — the golden hair that wiped her kisses and her tears from His beloved feet.

"Women have loved you, too, fantastic sinner, with a love as rich as Mary's. They have given you all they had. The labor of their hands. Every waking thought and worry of their minds. The beauty of their souls. Their very lives. You have repaid their love with love — but not such love as Mary wrung from Jesus.

"Follow her to the crypt, and be as great a saint!"

Christ brings new life from the tomb

There is incense in the tomb. And myrrh — a hundredweight of myrrh and aloes which Nicodemus had been saving for his own interment. There are spices and clean linens.

And now a stranger comes with gold, a stooped man with a mighty chest, who walks as though his ankles still were shackled, a man with black sharp eyes that lurk in the shadow of their lids and peer uneasily at strangers, a man with a beard uncombed and vicious.

He thrusts a purse into our Lady's hands and rubs a chafed place on his wrist.

"You were His mother, Lady. Don't be afraid of me, nor of these yellow images of Caesar. I am Barabbas, Lady, but I had no part in this. If I have blood upon me — oh, I have plundered caravans and slit the throats of merchants — if I have blood upon me, 'tis not His. I do not have to wash it from me as did Pilate. And the gold is clean. It was a gift I had from Dismas, my friend who died with Him."

"I give thee thanks, Barabbas," the Virgin answers him. "It is a gift of love. I will accept it."

"Love?" Barabbas bows his shaggy head and bends his shoulders. "I saw Him only once. We shared a cell together."

He disappears. And others take his place. The sick, the lame, the halt, the unclean, the blind, the crippled. There are so many there that Nicodemus calls to them, "Begone!"

"Nay, let them come," our Mother bids him. "All those who seek me I will comfort. All those who speak my name I will attend."

They pass, and others come. The tomb takes other shapes.

A sailor on a flaming ship lifts up his eyes to her, and she extends her arms in welcome. A soldier dying in the desert sands invokes her aid, and feels her hand touch his. A flyer in a falling plane cries, "Mary" and hears her say, "My son!"

St. Vincent de Paul emerges from the darkness with a baby in each arm.

"These orphans, Blessed Mother, need your care."

"Forever and forever, in life and death, I'll guard them," Mary promises.

A woman in a small white church moans piteously of loss.

"Your loved one is with God," our Lady chides her. "Rejoice, poor child. Give me your sorrow."

Before a wayside shrine a girl kneels, sobbing.

"O Mother Immaculate, I have sinned. Ask Jesus to forgive me."

The hand that soothed the Infant Savior when He cried, consoles the wayward girl.

"Mother, if I could only see Him," a nun prays in her cell.

"Ah, you shall see Him soon. He grows impatient for the wedding."

An old man on his deathbed quakes with terror, gazing upon a medal that someone had given him. "Is it too late?" his mind is asking. "Mary, Mother of God, is it too late?"

"Fear not," she comforts him. "God will be gentle."

Sisters in a chapel pray for the end of wars.

"O you who stand beside me at the Cross," I hear her whisper, "can you not understand there will be wars so long as men hate God? Do you not realize that only Love redeemed the world; and only Love can save it?"

A group of children sing to her in school. She smiles and blesses them.

And the tomb is dark again. Black night is charging fast against the sun-stained West.

Our Lady leaves the tomb without a backward glance. She holds the crown of thorns. And the bent and twisted nails. She does not see Barabbas roll the rock against the tomb.

"His crown!" she says. "True crown for Him, the King of Kings. And many of His heirs shall wear it in their time. Those He loves best, whom He would honor.

"How blest are they who wear a crown of thorns!"

She entrusts it to St. John.

"Handle it carefully, my Son. It is the only earthly treasure He has left us — save these nails."

Against her palms the nails are ugly, huge, mis-shapen symbols of barbarity and fear.

"They pierced His hands," she says. "They pierced the wood. Yet they went deeper than the wood. They pierced the world. They pierced the hearts of men — these holy nails.

"We have released Him from the wood. We have taken down the nails. Yet still they hold Him firmly, hand and foot, upon His Cross. I hold them in my hand yet they remain forever in the Cross, holding their Lord."

The sun has disappeared. It is the holy day. The soldiers stand on guard outside the tomb. And three women and three men toil slowly up the hill.

Of all the crowds who followed Jesus, only these few have followed to the end.

Christ brings new life from the tomb

"How often have we buried Jesus in the granite of our hearts!" laments the nun beside me. "How often have we rolled a stone against the door, that it might never open — that we might forget the Lord and His commandments! How often have we posted sentries at the tomb, to keep Him dead, and hidden from our timid consciences!"

The strutting soldiers anger her.

"Armor and arms that gleam with malice in the moonlight!" she exclaims. "Weapons to guard the shrine where Love lies scourged and slain! Hate, equipped and trained to keep the world from Love!

"Love, defeated, crawls the slope of Calvary, as He did. Love, bent, and heavily laden, climbs wearily upward to the blazing stars. How beautiful — and how forsaken!

"Aye, my Lord, my God, my Love is dead and buried. The tomb is sealed. Armed might protects the stone that shuts Him from me. But what is that to Him? He will arise in splendor and in power, let the world do what it will."

Our Lady has gained the Cross, and leans against it, seeking strength there for her weakness, and ease for her incalculable pain.

And now, miraculously, I need no one to weep by proxy for me. For, from my tearless eyes warm tears are streaking down my cheeks.

"If she could know her Son will rise up from the dead" — the thought occurs to me — "she need not feel this too sharp sword of sorrow."

"Our Lady knows that He will raise Himself on the third day," the blessed nun assures me. "But the knowledge is buried deep beneath an avalanche of anguish. Her poor numbed mind gropes feebly for that knowledge, Blindman, but will find only pain."

Once, I remember, when she had searched Judea for Him, I sent the saints to comfort her and find Him. Now let me send them as glad messengers of Easter, that she may nevermore know anything but joy.

I call the beautiful ladies of His court, the heroines of Heaven.

"Agnes, Ursula, Martha, Lucy."

My tongue grows stronger as I name their names. "Cecilia, Charlotte, Paula, Rose." My tongue grows sweeter. "Philomena, Gemma, Kateri Tekakwitha, Mohawk lily. Ta-juen Wang, the rose of China. Theresa, Frances, Gertrude, Clare."

I see them sifting earthward through the stars.

Christ brings new life from the tomb

"Monica, Martina, Agatha, Joan of Arc, Perpetua, Felicity, Anastasia, Dorothy, Anne, and Rita, and all you Catherines, Janes, Elizabeths, and Marys,

"See your queen on Calvary, mourning at the lonely Cross. Hasten to her, singing, with the news of Easter morn."

I hear them now. And feel the rapture of their souls.

"O Queen of heaven, rejoice. *Alleluia!*
For He Whom you did merit to bear.
Alleluia!
Has risen, as He said! *Alleluia!*"

They cluster about her, like stars around her head.

And the Archangel Gabriel kneels before her, as long ago he knelt, saying again, "Hail, Mary, full of Grace, the Lord is with you."

I say it over and over to myself, here at the tomb of Jesus, watching the miracle of light that floods our Lady's face — and waiting for the resurrection in my heart.

*The Rosary of the
Seven Sorrows of Our Lady*

The Rosary of the Seven Sorrows (the Servite Rosary) was developed in the Middle Ages for the ordinary Catholic who might not have been able to say the official daily prayer of the Church. It invites us to meditate on those times in the life of Mary when she was called in her unique way into the pain of the mystery of God's salvation as the Mother of her Son, Jesus.

Following each meditation, pray one Our Father and seven Hail Marys.

The First Sorrow: The prophecy of Simeon

Many of us are parents. We know that only by sharing life with God is life fulfilled. That is why we joyfully present our children to Him in Baptism, although we also sense a fear about the future of our loved ones. Simeon's prophecy was a blessing for all men and women, but foretold grief for you, Mary. Your first sorrow was much more than a parent's fear.

⁊

The Second Sorrow: The flight into Egypt

What can a mother do when her child's life is threatened? When Herod decreed death for all those innocent children, God warned Joseph. With no time for packing or goodbyes, you escaped into the night. Homeless, tired, with an uncertain future before you, you were secure in nothing but the love of those who needed you.

⁊

The Third Sorrow: Jesus is lost in the Temple

A child is lost. What panic grips the hearts of parents at such a time! They wonder, "Is he safe?" "Will I ever see him again?" And then they imagine things too terrible to express. It was the same for you and Joseph. Mary, for three days you sought Jesus. It took faith to continue the search in the pain of separation.

⁊

The Fourth Sorrow: The Way of the Cross

What mother called suddenly to the hospital to see her sick or injured child has not wished, "If only I could suffer instead of you!" But she remains only a spectator. Mary, you saw Jesus beaten and bloody. You felt powerless to help Him, and yet through your love you shared His pain.

⤳

The Fifth Sorrow: The Crucifixion

It has often been said, "To lose a child is the worst death for a parent to endure." Mary, in those long hours at the Cross, perhaps your thoughts returned to earlier days. How horrible now to face the reality of death! His breath grew labored. The time had come. Yet He spoke to you and consoled you. In dying He gave life to others and made you mother of all.

⤳

The Sixth Sorrow: Jesus is taken down from the Cross

He is dead . . . and it hardly seems real. How many of us have paused before the body of a loved one and wondered, "Can this be happening to me?" Death is real, all too real! As you held Jesus in your arms, Mary, you probably wondered as we have, "Is this the end of everything?"

⤳

The Seventh Sorrow: Jesus is laid in the tomb

The garden and the tomb . . . there is something strangely consoling about the burial of Jesus, Mary.

Splendor of Sorrow

Perhaps a flower or blade of grass reminded you of His words: "Unless a seed falls to the ground and dies, it cannot produce new life."[20] It is always difficult to see death and life together, but you continued to believe, hope, and love. His words filled your heart.

Closing Prayer

Lord God, our Father, from the Passion and death of Jesus, shared by the compassion of His Mother, you brought healing to the fallen.

Grant that we, your people, may experience this healing and rise from the power of sin to a wholeness of life promised by Jesus, who lives and reigns with you and the Holy Spirit, now and forever, Amen.

(Three Hail Marys)

---

[20] Cf. John 12:24-25.

Eddie Doherty
(1890-1975)

A hard-boiled reporter who wrote books with titles such as *Broadway Murders* and *Dark Masquerade* and who spent his old age as a Catholic priest, the colorful Eddie Doherty is a marvelous witness to the transforming power of God's grace.

Eddie was born into a large Irish Catholic family in Chicago in 1890. A self-described "happy-go-lucky sort of kid," his varied childhood interests foreshadowed the many twists and turns of his adult life. He was fond of books, sports, and serving at Mass; he dreamed of being a poet, the world's greatest heavyweight fighter, and a priest.

At the age of thirteen, he put aside his literary and sports aspirations and entered a Servite Monastery in Granville, Wisconsin, to pursue a priestly vocation, but in time he came to see the beauty of the vocation of marriage.

Splendor of Sorrow

Eddie left the monastery and took a job as a late-night police-beat reporter with the *Chicago Tribune*. Later he joined the *Chicago American* as a daytime reporter. He quickly made a name for himself as a writer: Eddie was smart, imaginative, and charming, and it seemed as if his successes were only beginning.

With his professional career soaring, Eddie solidified his personal life by marrying his childhood sweetheart, Marie Ryan. But only eighteen months after the birth of their son, Eddie Jr., in 1917, Marie was gone — killed in the great flu epidemic that swept across the nation in those days.

"When she died, her hand in mine," Eddie wrote, "I cursed God bitterly and violently," and he left the Catholic Church. Even when he later decided to reconcile with God, he still couldn't bring himself to go back into a Catholic church.

Eddie returned to the *Tribune* and, in 1919, secretly wed *American* reporter Mildred Frisby in a Protestant ceremony. They continued to live in separate homes until Mildred found that she was expecting a baby — a son, Jack Jim. Eddie wished to have their marriage blessed by the Church, but the priest they approached rebuked them severely for having married outside the

Church. Eddie thereupon once again turned his back on the Catholic Church.

His star as a reporter continued to rise as Eddie covered the likes of Al Capone and lesser thugs with great flair. In 1924, the family moved to New York City, where Eddie wrote for the *New York News* and became city editor for the *New York American*. It was a time of great success and high excitement for him. He enjoyed large salaries and covered history-making events, such as Charles Lindbergh's triumphant welcome to New York.

But even at the height of his worldly success, Eddie was still being pursued by the Hound of Heaven. In 1934, he attempted to gain an interview with the famous radio priest Fr. Charles Coughlin; in preparation, he read the autobiography of St. Thérèse of Lisieux. Greatly moved by the book and considering returning to the Church, he sought St. Thérèse's intercession to get an interview with Fr. Coughlin. Within hours, the priest offered to give Eddie an exclusive interview — provided he return to the Church. Eddie agreed. He attended Mass each Sunday, but didn't receive Communion, since he and Mildred had not had their marriage blessed by the Church.

Splendor of Sorrow

In 1939, Mildred fell to her death down a steep hillside while the couple was visiting California. Eddie, grieving deeply, did not curse God this time — instead, he began again to receive Holy Communion.

In 1940, while collecting material for a story on Harlem, Eddie discovered Friendship House, a Catholic lay apostolate directed by the Russian aristocrat Catherine de Hueck. He admired the devotion of Catholic laypersons there who served the poor, and he was fascinated by Catherine — so fascinated that he wrote a book about her called *Tumbleweed*.

For several years, he went to great lengths in pursuit of her hand, but met with firm refusals. Finally, in 1943, after he had spent several months in California writing the screenplay for the movie *The Fighting Sullivans*, he persuaded Catherine to marry him. Eddie promised to live, like Catherine, in voluntary poverty, but their marriage caused resentment among the staff at Friendship House, who lived in celibacy. Eddie and Catherine rented a modest apartment, and Eddie gave away all his possessions and found work as a reporter for the *Chicago Sun*.

In 1947, after Eddie was laid off from the *Sun* and tensions grew great between Catherine and Friendship House, the couple moved to Combermere, Ontario, to begin a rural lay apostolate. They led a rustic life and started a monthly newspaper called *Restoration*. A Friendship House staff member joined them, and they began tending to the needs of their rural neighbors. Madonna House was born and began to grow: teachers, nurses, office workers, and students came to volunteer and to pray, sing, and work together. Catherine gave spiritual talks and encouraged them to perform even the smallest tasks out of love for God.

In 1951, the future Pope Paul VI suggested that the apostolate become a secular institute, whose members would make promises of poverty, chastity, and obedience. Eddie and Catherine, who were already living in voluntary poverty and in obedience to their spiritual director, decided to live also in celibate chastity.

As his faith deepened, Eddie's desire to become a priest returned, but he was denied Ordination in the Latin Rite because he was married. However, in 1968 he was ordained a priest of the Melkite Greek Catholic Church (a Byzantine Rite Church in communion with Rome) by his friend Archbishop Joseph Raya.

Eddie Doherty died in 1975.

"What is death?" he once wrote. "A summoning home. A divine welcome to a well-loved child. An everlasting kiss from God! Only those fear death who know not the Resurrection and the Life."

Truly Eddie Doherty could look beyond the world's sorrows and difficulties to see the Resurrection and the Life. It was this marvelous view that enabled him to live life to the full and, through his writings, to help readers do the same.

Holy souls mentioned

St. Agatha, virgin martyred in Sicily.

St. Agnes, Roman martyr.

St. Albert the Great (c. 1200-1280), medical theologian, philosopher, and scientist.

St. Aloysius Gonzaga (1568-1591), Jesuit who cared for plague victims.

St. Alphonsus Liguori (1696-1787), bishop, Doctor, writer, and founder of the Redemptorists.

St. Anastasia (d. c. 304), martyr at Sirmium.

Bl. André Bessette (1845-1937), Canadian Holy Cross brother who built St. Joseph's Oratory in Montreal.

St. Ann, mother of the Blessed Virgin Mary.

St. Anthony of Padua (1195-1231), Franciscan friar and Doctor of the Church.

Splendor of Sorrow

St. Augustine (354-430), Bishop of Hippo.

St. Benedict (c. 480-c. 547), abbot who founded the monastery of Monte Cassino.

St. Bernard (1090-1153), abbot and Doctor.

St. Catherine of Siena (1347-1380), Dominican tertiary.

St. Cecilia, second- or third-century martyr and patron saint of musicians.

St. Christopher (d. c. 251), martyr under Decius.

St. Clare (c. 1193-1253), foundress of the Poor Clares.

Curé d'Ars (1786-1859), St. John Vianney; patron saint of parish priests.

Father Damien (1840-1888), missionary priest who cared for lepers.

St. Dismas, the repentant criminal crucified with Christ and known as the "Good Thief."

St. Dominic (c. 1170-1221), founder of the Dominicans.

St. Dorothy: possibly St. Dorothea (d. 311), martyr under Diocletian.

St. Felicity, early Roman martyr.

St. Francis Xavier Cabrini (1850-1917), Italian-born foundress of the Missionary Sisters of the Sacred Heart at Codogno in Lombardy and of orphanages and hospitals in North and South America; first United States citizen to be canonized.

St. Francis of Assisi (1182-1226), founder of the Franciscans.

St. Francis Borgia (1510-1572), Duke of Gandia who became a Jesuit, established the order throughout western Europe, and sent missionaries to the Americas.

St. Francis de Sales (1567-1622), Bishop of Geneva, writer, and Doctor.

St. Francis Xavier (1506-1552), Jesuit missionary to the East Indies.

St. Gabriel, message-bearing archangel.

St. Gemma Galgani (1878-1903), Italian stigmatist.
St. Gertrude (1256-c. 1302), German mystic.

St. Ignatius of Loyola (1491-1556), founder of the Jesuits.

St. Jerome (c. 342-420), Doctor who translated the Bible into Latin.

St. Joachim, father of the Blessed Virgin Mary.

Brother Joachim, Trappist monk at Gethsemani Abbey, Kentucky.

St. Joan of Arc (1412-1431), French heroine who led the French army against English invaders and was burned to death for alleged heresy, but later declared innocent.

Splendor of Sorrow

St. John, Evangelist and one of the Twelve Apostles.

St. John Bosco (1815-1888), founder of the Salesians.

St. John Chrysostom (c. 347-407), Archbishop of Constantinople and Doctor; named Chrysostom, or "Golden Mouth" for his eloquent preaching.

St. Juliana, martyr.

Bl. Kateri Tekakwitha (1656-1680), daughter of a Mohawk chief and a Christian mother who was baptized a Christian and cared for the sick and the elderly; known as the "Lily of the Mohawks."

St. Lucy (fourth century), virgin and martyr.

St. Margaret Mary Alacoque (1647-1690), Visitation nun who promoted devotion to the Sacred Heart of Jesus.

St. Martha, friend of Jesus and sister of Mary and Lazarus.

St. Martin de Porres (1579-1639), South American lay brother and infirmarian at the Dominican friary of the Rosary in Lima, Peru, and friend to the poor.

St. Martina (d. 228), martyr under Alexander Severus.

St. Michael, archangel who led God's army against Lucifer's uprising.

St. Monica (332-387), mother of St. Augustine.

St. Paula (347-404), widow who formed a community of religious women and helped St. Jerome in his biblical work.

Holy souls mentioned

St. Peregrine (1260-1345), convert to the Faith who became a Servite priest.

St. Perpetua, young married woman who was martyred in the third century.

St. Philip Benizi (1233-1285), Servite priest who worked for peace between the Guelphs and the Ghibellines and assisted at the second general Council of Lyons.

St. Philomena, early-Church martyr.

St. Rita of Cascia (1381-1457), widow who became an Augustinian nun who experienced ecstasies while meditating on our Lord's Passion.

St. Rose of Lima (1586-1617), third order Dominican and first canonized saint of the New World.

St. Thérèse of Lisieux (1873-1897), Carmelite nun and Doctor.

St. Thomas Aquinas (c. 1225-1274), Dominican philosopher, theologian, and Doctor.

St. Ursula, martyr and founder of the Ursulines.

St. Viator (d. c. 78), Bishop of Bergamo.

St. Vincent de Paul (1580-1660), founder of the Lazarist Fathers and the Sisters of Charity.

Sophia Institute™ is a nonprofit institution that seeks to restore man's knowledge of eternal truth, including man's knowledge of his own nature, his relation to other persons, and his relation to God.

Sophia Institute Press® serves this end in numerous ways: it publishes translations of foreign works to make them accessible for the first time to English-speaking readers; it brings out-of-print books back into print; and it publishes important new books that fulfill the ideals of Sophia Institute™. These books afford readers a rich source of the enduring wisdom of mankind.

Sophia Institute Press® makes these high-quality books available to the general public by using advanced technology and by soliciting donations to subsidize its general publishing costs. Your generosity can help Sophia Institute Press® to provide the public with editions of works containing the enduring wisdom of the ages.

Please send your tax-deductible contribution to the address below. We also welcome your questions, comments, and suggestions.

For your free catalog, call:
Toll-free: 1-800-888-9344

or write:
Sophia Institute Press®
Box 5284, Manchester, NH 03108

or visit our website:
www.sophiainstitute.com

Sophia Institute™ is a tax-exempt institution
as defined by the Internal Revenue Code,
Section 501(c)(3). Tax I.D. 22-2548708.